Engendering Democracy

For my parents, Margaret and Frederick Phillips

Engendering Democracy

Anne Phillips

The Pennsylvania State University Press
University Park, Pennsylvania

Copyright © Anne Phillips 1991

Originating publisher, Polity Press, Cambridge

First published 1991 in the United States of America by The Pennsylvania State
University Press, Suite C, 820 North University Drive, University Park, PA 16802.

0-271-00783-4 (cloth)
0-271-00784-2 (paper)

Library of Congress Cataloging in Publication Data
A CIP catalogue record for this book is available from the Library of Congress.

Typeset in 10½ on 12 pt Palatino
by Acorn Bookwork, Salisbury
Printed in Great Britain by T.J. Press

CONTENTS

ACKNOWLEDGEMENTS

This book has developed out of years of discussion and debate, and I cannot begin to acknowledge all those who have influenced me. But for their comments on earlier versions, I would like to thank Michèle Barrett, Ciaran Driver, Philip Green, Sophie Watson and Iris Young, none of whom of course should be held in any way responsible for the results. My editor David Held was a great help in pushing me to improve on my first draft. City of London Polytechnic provided me with generous research time for working on this book, for which I am immensely grateful.

1

FEMINISM AND DEMOCRACY

Democracy has existed as either nightmare or dream for as long as political thought. Feminism has been with us a much shorter period, and many commentators place its origins in seventeenth-century Europe. The two traditions have much in common for both deal in notions of equality and both oppose arbitrary power, but they did not develop in tandem: though ideals of equality might be thought to unite them, this has not proved any automatic bond. The ancient Greeks could conceive of democracy without any qualms about excluding both women and slaves; early liberals could talk of human beings as equals without any inkling that they might all expect to vote. The association between equality and democracy is itself a recent affair, and so inevitably is the relationship between feminism and democracy. In 1700, Mary Astell made the now obvious connection when she asked why those who so vehemently rejected the absolute sovereignty of a king nonetheless accepted it as natural in a husband. Being a dedicated royalist, she used the parallel to ironic effect. Ninety years later, the more politically radical Mary Wollstonecraft still knew she would 'excite laughter, by dropping a hint . . . that women ought to have representatives, instead of being arbitrarily governed without having any direct share allowed them in the deliberations of government' (1975:259–60). She pursued the issue no further. Early feminists recognized a link between feminism and democracy, but were preoccupied by more pressing concerns.

It was not till the nineteenth century, when a long history of discussion and writing began to coalesce into an active movement, that women demanded democratic rights for themselves. From this point onwards, the links with the democratic tradition steadily strengthened, though the belief that the two movements were related proved stronger on the feminist side. In our own period, the contemporary women's movement has forged a particularly powerful connection and, with its determined critique of hierarchy and sustained anti-authoritarianism, turned itself into a virtual testing ground for democracy's most radical ideals. For this reason, if no other, there is a wealth of experience to explore in the relationship between the two traditions. The democracy of the women's movement is one part of what this book is about.

But there is more to the relationship than that. It is a central contention in my argument that gender challenges all our political perspectives, forcing us to examine each position and concept afresh. Despite a growing weight of feminist critique, political theory has remained largely impervious to this. In political theory (as in virtually every field of enquiry) there has been a procession of competing traditions; though each age has tended to converge on one as the dominant or 'orthodox' approach, this has taken place through wide-ranging discussion and debate. In these controversies, political thinkers draw on a wealth of moral, psychological and historical argument, and might seem to agree on only one thing: whatever else is at stake, gender is irrelevant to the issues and will not affect the arguments on anyone's side.

With the odd exception, the entire debate on democracy has proceeded for centuries as if women were not there, or it has, as with Rousseau, only acknowledged us to show us our place. Contemporary writers usually comment at least briefly on this (not too long ago, they wouldn't even have noticed), but the presumption is that this is merely a scandalous oversight, and even then an understandable one. It has been left to feminists to explore how far the relentless privileging, not just of real living men, but of the very category of the male itself, has formed and deformed political theory and practice. And at one level it seems almost too obvious for argument that inserting women into the previously 'gender-neutral' (for which read male-defined) pre-occupations of political theory will prove a qualitative as well as a quantitative change.

It is bad enough that women were overlooked in the calls for freedom, equality and that all-too-precisely named 'rights of man': equally worrying in an ostensibly fairer age is that women are excluded from the theory even when acknowledged in the official demands. Early political theorists developed a variety of explicit arguments to justify their misogyny, but later writers seemed to take women's unworthiness so much for granted that they did not even notice they were leaving them out. In virtually the entire repertoire of what Mary O'Brien (1981) dubs 'male-stream' theory, women have been excluded or ignored or sub-sumed under men, and instead of treating this as a bit of unfinished labour, many feminists now see sexual inequality as something built into the very foundations of both classical and contemporary thought. If this is so, then the tasks of reconstruc-tion are more major than most (male) theorists had hoped. Politics has to be reconceptualized without the blindspots of gender and democracy rethought with both sexes written in. Old concepts must be fashioned anew.

This is a challenging position to take, but the ambition of the argument is not unique to women: it is arguably the mark of an emancipatory politics that it sets out some similar claim. People rarely make their bids for equality on the grounds of justice alone but, with a canny eye to the limits of moral persuasion, mostly keep another card up their sleeve. This can range from the strictly utilitarian (society has deprived itself unnecessarily of a reservoir of talent) to the grimmer warnings of imminent chaos (you will not keep the lid on our aspirations for long). One version that has proved repeatedly attractive presents the dispossessed as the answer to society's problems and sees their very subordination as giving them privileged access to the truth. Karl Marx made much of this in his theory of the proletariat as a universal class, and contemporary feminists have developed similar themes. Excluded first overtly and then more subtly from the ranks of full citizens, women have pressed their demands not just as a matter of justice, but in the name of a vision that transforms the world. Either positively as the bearers of new values and perspectives, or more negatively as a silenced and thwarted majority, they have per-ceived themselves as bringing something new to the political stage. Their much-delayed entry will not only add to the dramatis personae, but of necessity alter the play.

Both politically and theoretically, this sets a major test for orthodox views. Feminists have argued that women are kept out of politics by a series of powerful conventions that distinguish sharply between public and private. This separation has seriously

curtailed the range and content of public affairs, and has con-
signed to the private all the supposedly petty concerns of ordinary
life. Women's intimate association with childbirth and nurture is
said to restore the more appropriate dimensions: sharpening an
awareness of the devastations of war; strengthening concern for
the young, sick and old; grounding the abstractions of economic
or foreign policy in a more compassionate understanding of daily
need. The frequently presumed association between feminism
and peace politics is only one example of this.

In form as well as content, women have promised to radicalize
the very practices of democracy: to cut through the pomposity of
male rhetoric; to subvert unnecessary hierarchies; to open up
decision-making to those who were once objects of policy; to
create the world anew. There is a millenarian edge to this which
can make the most dedicated uneasy, and within the wide spectrum of feminist thought, there is disagreement and debate
between those who occupy different extremes. There have been
moments of pragmatism – as when anti-suffragists argued that
women would just vote the same way as 'their' men, and were
then asked, so why on earth not let them do it? But most supporters of women's equality cherish a belief that the changes they
desire have as much a qualitative as a quantitative side. It is not
just a matter of more women in politics; it is a chance of transforming the political realm.

In more philosophical vein, feminist writers have suggested
that women have a different conception of power (Hartsock 1983);
that they have a different system of morality (Gilligan 1982); and
they have argued that some of the most fundamental categories of
contemporary thinking – the concept of the individual (Pateman
1988, 1989), the notion of interests (Diamond and Hartsock 1981),
the assumption that equality means similar treatment (Eisenstein
1989) – are derived from a masculine mode. The gloomy sense that
no one will listen is thus partially offset by the confidence in what
feminists have to say, and there is a growing consensus that this
shakes the foundations of previous debate. There are always those
who take a more sober view, arguing like Judith Evans that 'the
bias exists in the assumptions of political theorists, but not in the
techniques which they employ' (1986:1). In the literature of today,
this seems a minority stance. Most contemporary feminists see
themselves as taking on framework and techniques as well as the
content, and expect very little to survive intact.

Despite this increasingly confident consensus, an important

distinction has emerged: between those who anticipate the development of a genuinely gender-free theory, and those for whom sexual difference is a necessary and substantive divide. Feminists have always disagreed – between themselves and often enough within themselves – about whether to press for a world in which sex becomes irrelevant, or to argue for a future in which sexual difference no longer acts as a basis for making us unequal. Translated into the patterns of contemporary political theory, this takes the form of an argument over universal concepts and goals. Beginning with such works as Susan Moller Okin's *Women in Western Political Thought*, continuing through major contributions by such writers as Jean Bethke Elshtain, Carole Pateman, Mary Dietz and Iris Marion Young, feminists have challenged the deceptive abstractions of classical and contemporary theory, and have revealed these as being thoroughly saturated by sex. What at first seemed an absence becomes on closer examination an unspoken but powerful presence, for under the seemingly innocent guise of gender neutrality, masculinity has defined the terms. Political theorists have conducted their trade in terms that deliberately abstract from the pettiness of everyday life, or the accidents of gender and class, but in doing so they have taken one sex alone as their standard, forcing the other one to conform or be damned.

Though feminists have a long way to go in convincing others of the scale of this deception, the real issues for feminism arise over what to do next. One possibility is to take the proclaimed universalism of political theory seriously, to reveal the myriad ways in which it has fallen short of its supposed neutrality, to push it onwards to its gender-free goal. This is a mammoth task in itself and one on which much work is currently being done. An increasingly prominent alternative presents universality as itself a fraud. Introducing the collection *Feminist Challenges* (Pateman and Gross 1986), Carole Pateman notes that though the editors provided only general guidelines, the contributions were strikingly at one in their themes and concerns. None of them had much time for what she calls 'domesticated feminism': that tamest of versions that sees women and the relations between the sexes as something to be incorporated into existing ideas and as posing no special theoretical problems of their own. The articles reflected instead a new consensus (on the problems if not also the answers) and Pateman was sufficiently emboldened by this agreement to venture a strong statement on what constitutes feminist theory. 'Distinctively feminist theory begins from the recognition that individuals are feminine and masculine, that individuality is not a unitary abstraction but an embodied and sexually differentiated expression of the unity of humankind' (p. 9). The problem then is not how to eliminate the old-fashioned bias by substituting concepts that are untainted by sex. Sexual difference will have to be admitted right into the theories, and this may mean redoing nearly all that has been done.

Such arguments are very much the mood of our time, for in an epoch that many characterize as postmodernist, the pretensions of totalizing theory are widely scrutinized. Feminism has already contributed to a loss of confidence in Marxism, and has pressed the claims of gender as something that operates independently of class. The analysis of women's experience and oppression has been felt to subvert the fundamental tenets of historical materialism, the definition of the economic, and the nature and meaning of power. Recent developments in feminist political theory now take this further. The humanism of the Enlightenment has come under general attack, not just for its over-confident expectations of progress but for its abstractions and universalizing claims. The certainty of much eighteenth-century or nineteenth-century thought seems distinctly odd to people today; threatened as modern societies have felt themselves to be by nuclear or environmental devastation, the movement of history often appears to have gone into reverse. More to the point perhaps, the very idea that there are stages of history has gone out of fashion, as have all those concepts – like History, Humanity, Reason – that used to attract capital letters. The current feminist preoccupation with heterogeneity and difference combines easily with this, for arguments that highlight the 'man' in humanity lead on to more general scepticism over any universalizing claims.

The polarity between universal values and a sexually differentiated experience is the subtext around which I have written this book, and in exploring the intersection between feminist and democratic theory I have positioned myself between the two poles. As will become clear, I see the conventional assumption of a non-gendered, abstract citizenship as something that does indeed operate to centre the male. In denying the pertinence of gender, previous democratic theorists have reinforced the position of the sex that is historically dominant; in identifying politics with (a very particular definition of) the public sphere, they have made democracy coterminous with the activities that have been historically associated with men. In this sense, and to this extent, I am thoroughly in sympathy with those who highlight sexual differ-ence and who challenge the presumption that politics should stand above sex. There are two obvious implications that flow from this perspective, and I argue for both in this book. The first is to develop representative mechanisms that explicitly acknowledge gender difference and gender inequality, and in this way ensure a new proportionality between the sexes in those arenas within which political decisions are made. The second is to build on the insights of women's movement politics to reorder the relationship between public and private spheres.

Underlying this, however, is a vision of a world in which gender should become less relevant and the abstractions of humanity more meaningful, through our actions as well as our words. I regard the emphasis on sexual differentiation as neces-sary, but transitional, for I do not want a world in which women have to speak continuously as women – or men are left to speak as men. Those who have been previously subordinated, marginal-ized or silenced need the security of a guaranteed voice and, in the transitional period to a full and equal citizenship, democracies must act to redress the imbalance that centuries of oppression have wrought. But I cannot see this as other than a version of 'affirmative action'. The proposed changes justify themselves by past bad behaviour, but they look forward to a future when such procedures become redundant, when people are no longer defined through their nature as women or men. In this future scenario, the distinction between public and private spheres would have lost its gendered quality. Men and women would move equally between the responsibilities of household and employment, would share equally in bringing up children and caring for parents, would vary as individuals rather than sexes in their priorities or experience, and would be equally attracted to (or repulsed by!) a political life. In such a context, the notion of the citizen could begin to assume its full meaning, and people could participate as equals in deciding their common goals.

What makes this controversial is, first, the theoretical assump-tions that underlie any reference to abstract humanity, universal values or common goals; and, second, the practical implications of acting as if a period is transitional when each of us knows it will last out our life. The theoretical issues will reappear later in the book, so let me just say something on the more overtly political concern. I suspect that a majority of contemporary feminists would share my vision of a desirable future, but many would query the apparent implication that such a future could be readily attained. If sexual difference continues to be a major organizing principle of society as we know and loathe it, what kind of hostage to fortune do I give in suggesting that difference is something that ultimately we 'ought' to transcend? How close does this slide towards confirming women's difference as the problem, rather than taking it as given and calling on the theories and the policies to adjust?

In my more lucid moments, I do not know the answer to this question, which shares with all the major political conundrums the difficult relationship between the tasks we might set ourselves for the present and the visions we cling to of our longer term goals. The ideals of democracy propel us, however, in two directions. Once they have been informed by a feminist perspective, they call on us to take seriously the many ways in which sexual difference has thwarted the promises of democratic equality, and instead of sweeping this under the carpet with a rhetoric of free and equal citizenship, to construct a democracy that can be meaningful to both sexes. Yet the ideals of democracy also raise expectations of a politics in which people will no longer be locked into their own specific or localized concerns, but will participate with other members of their community in reaching decisions that are mutually acceptable, on matters that are common to all. The first aspect stresses sexual difference as something potentially positive, and something we must not ignore. The second treats difference as a potential constraint.

It is this second aspect that has provoked so much criticism of the liberal tradition, for liberal democracy tends to assume that each individual (for the twentieth-century theorists of pluralism, substitute 'group') will pursue his or her private preferences, interests and needs, and that the best we can hope for is to register these and add them up. For those democrats – myself included – who dream of a more engaged and active democracy, this seems a sorry retreat. One would like to think of people as able to enter into, understand, but also challenge, the varying perspectives that derive from different experiences, and not be confined to expressing their own individual or group needs. This is not to say they should put their personal experience or group interest out of their minds, or that they should act as abstract citizens and forget everything that has made them 'different'. But it does suggest a certain ambivalence towards sexual, as indeed any kind of difference. No democracy can claim to be equal while it pretends away what are major and continuing divides; yet democracy is lessened if it treats us *only* in our identities as women or men. I want to keep both these aspects firmly in mind.

The problems of democracy So what are the 'problems of democracy'? When I began writing this book, I thought of democracy as something we all aspired towards, yet something on which no one had very much to say. 'We are all democrats today,' notes John Dunn in his review of Western political theory (1979:1); and perhaps because of this, the theorists mostly busied themselves elsewhere. For much of the 1970s and 1980s, the names most repeatedly cited as the leading political thinkers of the time were Robert Nozick and John Rawls, neither of whom has had much to say about the problems of the democratic process. The issues they address concentrate on the appropriate relationship between individuals and the state: the principles that determine what a state can or should do. Thus Nozick (1974) argues for a minimal state in which the rights of the individual are absolutely inviolate; Rawls (1971) for principles of redistributive justice that will keep inequality to an acceptable level. Neither is concerned with the stuff of politics in the sense of the ways in which decisions are made. Rawls provides guidelines for the *content* of political decisions (to what extent can the state justifiably interfere with the distribution of income?) rather than the practices of decision-making, while Nozick so severely restricts the role of the state as to make issues of representation a merely academic concern.

Attracted by the possibilities for rigorous analysis and critical sophistication, political theorists devoted much energy to criticism, refinement and reassessment (see, for example, the essays in Daniels (1975) and Paul (1982). Democratic theory could boast no parallel appeal for, instead of holding out these joys of abstract thought, it still seemed the terrain of the emotionally charged. Democracy was a battleground for optimists and pessimists, with considerable evidence on the paucity of our achievements and all too little to demonstrate the viability of anything more. In the twentieth-century literature, we have survived (not quite intact) a hard-nosed realism that has tried to break us of utopian dreams, and the questions posed *en route* can appear too classic to inspire novel ideas. What is the basic minimum below which no political system must fall if it is to describe itself as democratic? And how far can we move above this minimum without setting in motion forces that will go on to defeat the democratic ideal?

The minimum that most people would now identify is that governments should be elected and all adults have the equal right to vote. This minimum is itself a recent and fragile achievement, even in Britain, where it was not until 1928 that women over twenty-one gained the right to vote on the same basis as men, and in the United States, where it was not until the fierce contests of the civil rights movement in the 1950s and 1960s that black people were able to register their right to vote on the same basis as white people. In 1989, Eastern Europe erupted in a series of democratic revolutions, where in one country after another the key demand was for free elections and multi-party competition: the right to democracy as practised in the West. In China in the same year an apparently similar movement towards increased democracy was violently crushed; in many of the countries in Africa, Latin America and Asia, military regimes rule. The principle of equal rights to vote and choose one's government is vitally important, and is enjoyed by only a minority in the world.

Yet the minimum is also so very minimal, and long before the realization of full adult suffrage in Western Europe, Jean-Jacques Rousseau poured out his fulsome contempt: 'The English people believes itself to be free; it is gravely mistaken; it is free only during the election of Members of Parliament; as soon as the Members are elected, the people is enslaved; it is nothing' (1968: 141). What kind of accountability is it that operates only once every four or five years? What kind of choice is it that can select only more of the same?

The limits of representative democracy have been exhaustively canvassed in the course of the twentieth century, and even those who most vigorously defend it have tended to say that it is just the best we can hope to achieve. Full adult suffrage and periodic elections seem to combine happily with rule by a few, and for decades those defending the status quo occupied the impoverished ground that we do at least choose between competing elites. For those kept out of *any* elite, this may not seem much of a deal, but their aspirations were then subdued by the second major defence of the status quo. Further democratization, it was argued, is counter-productive. The 'people' are too irrational to be trusted with power; let us be thankful for the apathy that keeps them passive and quiet. Joseph Schumpeter (1942) was one of the earlier exponents of this dismal view. He thought that even writing to MPs should be discouraged, for though democracy indicates a certain level of popular control (representatives should submit to periodic elections) it would be threatened by anything more. For those of his generation, the experience of fascism served as a powerful reminder that whatever the limits of defining democracy by periodic elections, these were far preferable to what gets put in its place. Greater participation might look an attractive option, but the consequences were thought to be dire.

Among European and American radicals, the main burst of enthusiasm for wider democracy came in the 1960s, when fascism had retreated into the shadows and liberal democracy seemed all too securely in place. The complacencies of the latter were dismissed and, reclaiming the tradition of direct democracy that had its last major exponent in Rousseau, the student movement and New Left put participation once more on the map. Political parties were said to offer only shades in a consensus; elections only fooled us into believing we were free. In a ferment of discussion and action, people tried to assert more substantial control: (organizing demonstrations, setting up co-operatives, creating community action groups and workplace committees, trying to take decisions into their own hands. Neither liberal democracy nor its pluralist refinements held much counter-attraction, while representation was considered a pretty dubious affair. In an emphasis that overlapped with many of the practices of the contemporary women's movement, democracy was conceived in terms of the rough and tumble of the meeting rather than the anonymity of the ballot box, in terms of active participation rather than the passivities of the vote.

In a further point of contact with feminism, the supporters of participatory democracy usually moved beyond the traditional agenda, redefining what politics was about. Democracy was no longer thought of in terms of a (rather feeble) mechanism for controlling government, but as popular control in everyday life. Workplace democracy re-emerged as a central concern. In her influential *Participation and Democratic Theory*, Carole Pateman (1970) anticipated many of the enthusiams of the time when she discussed the achievements of worker self-management in Yugoslavia, arguing that it was through being involved in decisions at work that people would be empowered to participate in larger concerns. Community politics was the other explosive development, promoting active involvement in local decisions and challenging the remoteness of political life.

This division between representative and participatory democracy set the terms of debate, but for what many have considered a doomed discussion. John Dunn, for example, talks of the 'two distinct and developed democratic theories loose in the world today – one dismally ideological and the other fairly blatantly Utopian' (1979:26); the language he adopts to describe each camp shows he expects nothing new from this stale confrontation. Behind all the arguments that have been marshalled by each alternative, there lurks the suspicion that this is essentially a psychological divide: pessimists versus optimists, locked in a battle which no one can win. Everyone seems to want *some* democracy, but between the minimum and maximum, how do we begin to make up our minds? This is the point often reached in our thoughts on democracy, the moment when we shrug our shoulders and abandon the problems to some other day. Democracy has been beset by an endless series of contrasting pairs – bourgeois democracy versus socialist, liberal versus radical, representative versus direct, protective versus developmental (Macpherson), unitary versus adversary (Mansbridge), thin versus strong (Barber) – and in the growing vocabulary of opposites, each is open to reinterpretation as a matter of mere temperament or style. On the one side stand the sober-suited defenders of the status quo, minimalist, cautious, putting up with a little rather than risking what might mean losing the lot. On the other side, the wild-eyed visionaries, full of excitement and energy, but rarely thinking more than two steps ahead. If this is what the problems of democracy come down to, no wonder so many theorists decided to evacuate the field.

Some, fortunately, remained. Meanwhile democracy itself moved back to the centre of the political stage, with an accumulation of events in Poland, the Soviet Union, China, Hungary, East Germany, Czechoslovakia, Romania, that made the 1980s such an extraordinary decade. In both West and East, socialists began to make their peace with the institutions of parliamentary democracy, and the easy confidence with which radicals had dismissed representative democracy rapidly dissolved. Throughout the 1980s, there was mounting pressure for freedom of association, free elections and multi-party competition in the Eastern bloc. This combined with increased anxiety over infringements on individual rights and freedoms in the West, and, with the temporary exhaustion of the erstwhile practitioners of participatory democracy, the combination proved almost impossible to withstand. The dramatic events of 1989 made democracy the word on everyone's lips, even if it was democracy as minimally defined. The rights and freedoms that had once been derided by Western radicals now stood out as supremely important: the right to a (relatively) free press; the right to choose (more or less) between different parties; the right to dismiss a government in periodic elections. People put from their minds the desultory use so many have made of these rights, or the ease with which minorities have protected their interests long after the majority has claimed the vote. These rights and freedoms seemed worth dying for again.

As far as democratic theory is concerned, however, the main novelty has been that radicals now take seriously what used to be regarded as the liberal side. Concerning themselves more rigorously with the rights and freedoms of the individual, they stress the democracy of periodic elections. The authoritarian state has largely supplanted the powers of capital in the demonology of Western socialists, so much so that John Keane redefines socialism 'as a synonym for the democratic maintenance and transformation of the division between civil society and the state' (1988a:33). The individualism of the vote has replaced the groupiness of the meeting, while the 'fetish of direct democracy' (Bobbio 1986:78) has been put very firmly in its place. All these shifts in emphasis and priority represent a sea change for the radical and socialist traditions, but they do not necessarily advance our thinking on democracy itself. The reinstatement of liberal democracy as something positive (not just the best we can do) is one of the major theoretical phenomena of our time. But as long as this operates within the conventional pairings – when, for example, it reverses the previous preference so that liberal democracy now stands above radical, or representative becomes better than direct – it adds little to our understanding. I could put this more strongly, for it may reflect just another psychological quirk, that curious capacity for forgetting one set of problems once we become preoccupied with a new combination. The more substantial democracy of the participatory model is a potential casualty here.

Three models of democracy The importance of feminism is not that it will add its weight to one or other of two sides, but that its concerns might change the shape of the discussion. One obvious starting point is the fact that democracy has been so frequently presented as a choice between two opposing traditions, with the arguments revolving around some contrasting pair. Even without the feminist suspicion of dichotomy we might note something fishy in this. The idea that there is a single either/or choice recurs throughout the literature, and yet the different versions that have been developed cannot be substituted for each other at will. This slippage is most apparent when we take the contrast between bourgeois and socialist democracy, and set it alongside the contrast between liberal and radical democracy: there are quite different issues at stake. But even where the terms might seem more interchangeable, they do not simply or neatly overlap. The contrast between liberal and radical will not translate exactly into representative versus direct; nor into C. B. Macpherson's distinction between protective and developmental democracy; nor into Jane Mansbridge's distinction between adversary and unitary; nor into Benjamin Barber's distinction between thin and strong. The main consistency is political. All these oppositions set up an orthodoxy (which is liberal democracy, though variously defined) and then explore some alternative to this norm. There is however no consensus over what this alternative might be.

Benjamin Barber, for example, distinguishes his 'strong' democracy from liberal (thin) democracy, but also from 'the subterfuges of unitary democracy' (1984: 150) which lead people to presume they have a common interest, and end up with conformism and being coerced to consent. Jane Mansbridge (1980) stresses the adversary and conflictual nature of liberal democracy, but then counterposes it to a unitary democracy which takes as its premise mutual respect and common interest, and aspires to consensual decisions. Iris Young (1989) draws a contrast between liberal contractarianism and civic republicanism, highlighting not so much the way they differ over degrees of participation but more their different attitudes to 'public' life. The idea that there are two traditions repeatedly returns, but there is no consistency in the way each one gets described.

A number of writers have tried to challenge the hold of the binary opposition, and have stressed instead the variety of democratic 'models' (most recently, Held 1986). Feminists cannot therefore claim credit for discovering there is more than a two-way divide, and indeed I would be hard put to it to cite references where feminists have developed this point. That said, the emphasis the women's movement puts on the relationship between public and private spheres helps break the straitjacket of these endless pairings, for it draws our attention not only to the division between liberal and radical, but to a further subdivision within the radical camp.

As many critics comment, liberal democracy reflects a frightened kind of politics. It began in anxious anticipation of what governments might do, and, with the subsequent extension of democratic rights and suffrage, it ended up in fear of the people themselves. Its current emphasis on accountability through the ballot box is designed to meet both of these fears. Governments that have to present themselves regularly for electoral inspection will not dare exceed their allotted role, while constituents who are bound by the principles of majority rule will not be able to do anything too foolish. The other great principle running through this version of democracy is the separation between public and private spheres. Liberal democracy designates certain areas as outside governmental control, sometimes by formally establishing individual rights and freedoms in a written constitution but more commonly through historically shifting conventions over what can be considered a public concern. Whichever procedure operates the arm of government will be limited and kept away from the private domain.

Critics of liberal democracy have often homed in on the distinctions it makes between public and private, or what is sometimes but not always the same thing, the distinction between the political and the social. The limits that liberals put on government not only operate to protect individual freedoms, they also sustain a gross inequality that can make a mockery of democracy itself. The equal right to vote, for example, does not guarantee an equality of influence on political decisions, for the resources we bring to politics (money, contacts, education, time) disproportionately favour certain groups, while the economic or bureaucratic power of non-elected bodies (private companies being one obvious example, the civil service or executive branch another) is such that major decisions are made on their terms. Jean-Jacques Rousseau is famous for his argument that inequality in possessions undermines freedom and consent, that as long as one man is rich enough to make another his servant, and another so poor that he has to submit, we cannot talk of them as equally independent and free. Karl Marx saw the split between public and private, citizen and bourgeois, state and civil society as crucial underpinnings to liberal philosophy; in his essay *On The Jewish Question*, he excoriates the 'double life' we are then forced to lead. The fully developed liberal state 'abolishes' distinctions based on birth, rank, education, occupation (and by our own century even distinctions based on race and sex), but only in the sense that it declares them politically irrelevant. Granting us the universality of citizenship on

the one hand, liberalism simultaneously 'freed' us from any constraints on our 'private' affairs. It turned politics to the service of
egoistic and material concerns.

The school of thought normally described as participatory
democracy challenges the distinction between public and private
realms, arguing that if democracy matters in the state, it matters
just as much, if not more, elsewhere. Most typically, this
approach will stress the importance of workplace democracy.
People need and want to be involved in the decisions that directly
affect their lives. Thus, instead of excluding the factory or the
office as irrelevant – as private, non-political concerns – we should
think of democracy as something that builds up from work-based
participation. A more participatory democracy would transform
what for the moment is an uneasy relationship between political
and economic equality, for if workers were able to affect decisions
made at work, this would counter the influence of privileged
elites. But greater participation would be an issue even in a world
of economic equals: as Carol Gould argues, 'every person who
engages in a common activity with others has an equal right to
participate in making decisions concerning such activity' (1988:
84).

This is one direction from which radical democrats attack the
limited ambitions of liberal democracy, with arguments that seem
to dissolve the boundary between public and private realms. What
has been described as the tradition of civic republicanism or civic
humanism remains by contrast wedded to the public/private distinction. Most of its exponents have no interest in workplace
democracy – some are explicitly hostile – and while they share the
participationist's concern over the poverty and passivities of liberal democracy, they place no confidence in what they deem
'micro' participation. Drawing inspiration from the Greek city-
states, the republic of Rome, and Renaissance Italy, they conceive
of politics as a very special kind of affair that marks out the human
from the animal world. It is to this 'political animal', the citizen,
that they speak, not to the workers with their more 'private'
affairs. The great crime of liberalism was that it turned the activities of citizenship to the service of private interest or desires, and
emptied politics of its public importance. The solution is not to
spread democracy around, into more and more corners of our
everyday life, but to re-establish the political as what makes us
human and free.

I am thinking here not so much of the classical exponents of
republican ideals as of their twentieth-century heirs. There is a

long list of writers, perhaps most notably Hannah Arendt and Sheldon Wolin, who have identified the collapse of the public sphere as a central feature of the modern world, and who view the crisis of democracy largely in these terms. Arendt and Wolin draw on the experience of the ancient world to challenge the way that public space has been invaded by private interest, and note with regret the decline of a specifically political sphere. Without sharing Arendt's nostalgia for the past, Benjamin Barber reflects many of the same concerns in his critique of the liberal tradition. From a different but related perspective, Michael Sandel (1984) argues that modern states have become too large to operate as real communities and that, as it is communities that provide the context for any substantial notions of justice or morality, we have therefore been forced into the minimalist politics of protecting individual rights and ensuring just procedures: 'And so the gradual shift, in our own practices and institutions, from a public philosophy of common purposes to one of fair procedures, from a politics of good to a politics of rights, from the national republic to the procedural republic' (p. 93). The consequence, he suggests, is 'a tendency to crowd out democratic possibilities'; politics becomes less a matter of active citizenship and more just a question of rules.

The twentieth-century exponents of civic republicanism and participatory democracy share in a powerful critique of the liberal tradition, but approach this from different angles that reflect an almost continental divide. For much of Europe, the tradition of radical democracy developed in close association with socialist theory and practice. It derived its strength from the socialist critique of inequality, arguing that it was not enough to create 'political' equalities and rights. In the United States, however, radical democracy has been more typically influenced by a tradition of small town democracy, and its radicalism is less economically defined. What has most troubled writers in Europe is the contrast between political equality and economic subordination. What has most troubled writers in the USA (a country where voter turnout in presidential and congressional elections dropped below 50 per cent in the course of the 1970s) is the declining significance people attach to public affairs. In both contexts there is a debate between liberalism and its critics, but there is a three-way, not a two-way, divide.

I do not claim an exclusive insight here, but feminism has devoted so much attention to the relationship between public and private spheres that it has been impossible to write about feminism and democracy without at least noticing that there is more than one pair. When the issues of democracy are conceived in terms of a general rubric of participation (how much is possible or desirable? how often should we participate and where?) this blurs the contrast between participatory and republican models, for both of them envisage a more active democracy and challenge the minimalism of the liberal approach. It is when we add in gender that the picture becomes clearer. The different positions that democrats assume on the relationship between public and private spheres then seem as important as what they think about degrees of active involvement. United though they often are in their critical analysis of the liberal tradition, the 'participationists' and 'republicans' are at odds with each other over the public/private divide.

Feminist alternatives This then is my point of departure for exploring the relationship between feminist and democratic theory. Most of the contributions to contemporary debate can be attached to one or other of these three schools of thought – liberal democracy, participatory democracy, civic republicanism – and feminists have raised problems over each. Chapter 2 explores the traditions in turn. While the aim is partly to summarize and develop feminist critiques, the chapter also serves to remind the reader of problems and aspirations that have run through centuries of democratic debate. A number of points emerge: the peculiar significance of a participatory democracy that gives weight to activity and transformation; the conflict nonetheless between raising levels of participation and ensuring that all groups have an equal say; the choice between starting from group interests and perspectives or aspiring to a politics that transcends more local concerns. The tension between the universal and the particular is one recurrent theme, and in considering the implications of the recent feminist emphasis on sexual difference, I end with a modified defence of universal claims.

The rest of the book turns to the agenda that has been set by the women's movement: the under-representation of women in local and national politics; the de-gendering of the public/private divide; and the experience of the contemporary women's movement as a participatory democracy. The first of these deals with what for women is the most glaring of democracy's sins. Having lowered its sights to reasonable representation and occasional popular control, liberal democracy has nonetheless proved resistant to any substantial representation of women, and in most contemporary Western democracies, the number of women elected remains abysmally low. Various writers have explored the way in which women have achieved formal political equality without substantive political influence, and buried in what I once thought tedious empirical accounts of the number of women in politics are some crucial democratic concerns. Chapter 3 focuses on two of these. Women are obviously under-represented in the current composition of our national and local assemblies, but what exactly is the alternative we might want to propose? Increasing the proportion of women elected need not increase the representation of women *per se*, for it is only when there are mechanisms through which women can formulate their own policies or interests that we can really talk of their 'representation'. Many of the arguments for increasing the number of women in politics have blurred this key issue of accountability, yet a concern with accountability has become one of the signs by which a democrat can be known. There is potential confusion here, and a case for a more rigorous approach.

The literature on women and politics also offers fertile ground for exploring the extent to which political equality rests on substantial social or economic conditions, and this is the second question I pursue. For a small minority of countries, the last two decades have brought major changes in the representation of women; for others, they have brought just a bit more (or even less) of the same. The growing gap between the Nordic countries and the rest of Europe is particularly striking and has attracted considerable attention. The number of women now elected in Norway or Sweden or Denmark has reached levels that are almost inconceivable in Britain or the United States; and yet the position of women in their labour markets is not so different from anywhere else. Politics appears to be more of an independent variable than might have been expected and substantial political equalities look possible even in the absence of thoroughgoing social or economic reform. Despite its poor record in the past, liberal democracy may not be as antagonistic to women as previous evidence had seemed to show.

Chapter 4 looks at the relationship between public and private spheres, and deals with those issues most commonly cited as feminism's contribution to mainstream debate. There are many meanings attached to the idea that 'the personal is political' and most of these have implications for the way we think of democracy. The women's movement, for example, has stressed the relationship between means and ends, and highlighted the importance of what used to be dismissed as trivial detail, things outside of political concerns. This emphasis on the ways in which people relate to one another begins to dissolve distinctions of scale and kind, and sets a much higher standard against which democracies should be judged. The other aspect is the way that an emphasis on gender begins to dissolve distinctions of place, so that feminists join forces with the participatory school to query the boundaries between politics and the rest of our life. This extends the scope and relevance of democracy to fit every corner of our everyday life. In considering the consequences of this, I have been particularly concerned with the criticisms that would be levelled at this by democrats from the republican camp. Like most contemporary feminists, I end up arguing against simply dissolving the distinction between public and private spheres; perhaps more quirkily, I am influenced in my conclusions by notions of a revitalized 'public' life.

Chapter 5 considers the women's movement as an experience of participatory democracy. In tune with much of the radicalism of the 1960s and 1970s, the women's liberation movement launched a determined onslaught on hierarchies, criticized the divisions between leaders and led, and challenged the development of feminist 'stars'. Inside the movement, women worked to share out expertise and revolve positions of influence, while in their other engagements (trade unions, for example, tenants' associations, political parties) they developed a vision of grass roots involvement that would 'democratize everyday life'. In the choice between occasional forays into the polling booth and more continuous direct involvement, feminists undoubtedly placed themselves in the participatory camp. But this was not without debate, discontent and reassessment. The difficulties that developed were substantial, but as far as a movement is concerned they do not necessarily undermine the arguments for more equal and active involvement. The more troubling problems arise if this model of participation is extended to the level of the polity as a whole.

When a democracy sets high demands on people's activity and involvement, participation becomes a minority affair, posing a harsh choice between the intensity of involvement and the extent to which that participation is equally shared around. This is the dilemma of direct democracy and, despite the recent association between feminism and direct democracy, women's lives make the point more sharply than anything else. In societies where the division of labour is ordered by sex (that is, every society we know), time becomes a crucial constraint on women and meetings an additional burden. The inverse relationship between intensity of participation and numbers of participants is all too familiar to those who have been active in the women's movement, and the cycle which takes women out of politics during periods of caring for a child or parent has never escaped attention. Feminism brings to the problem of participatory democracy the most acute combination of reasons for wanting it to work, and reasons why it probably won't. Is there the beginnings of an answer in contemporary theory or practice?

Chapter 6 then draws together strands from the earlier sections, but organized through an explicit discussion of the possibilities and limits of liberal democracy. Feminism developed in close alliance with liberalism, and the liberal emphasis on individual autonomy and equal rights continues to inspire many women towards a feminist perspective. Yet as far as contemporary theory goes, the liberal tradition is frequently presented as inimical to the language and concepts of gender; and among those who have analysed liberal *democracy*, feminism is sometimes seen as dealing it the definitive blow. My own conclusions are less dramatic, and argue for an empowering democracy that nonetheless incorporates key elements of the liberal approach.

My starting point for the book as a whole is that feminism has major implications for the way we should think of democracy, but we cannot presume in advance that these will transform the very foundations of debate. The scale and ambition of contemporary feminist argument recall similar arguments made on behalf of the proletariat, whose emergence in the course of the nineteenth century likewise provided the ground for escalating claims. From the seemingly incontrovertible point that production is class-based, Marx derived a new theory of political economy; from the critique of liberal individualism, a version of equality that was antithetical to the principle of rights; from the critique of liberal democracy, a profound challenge to parliamentary forms. In the subsequent elaboration of the Marxist and socialist traditions, there was virtually no issue in politics, economics or philosophy that failed to produce its novel response: the world of theory was revolutionized and orthodoxy knocked on its head.

Marxism – like much contemporary feminism – presented itself as able to transcend previous dichotomies: between the individual and society, the universal and the particular, the abstract and the concrete, freedom and determination. Unlike feminism, Marxism is now in theoretical retreat and recent writing displays a marked predeliction for what used to be the bane of socialist thought. I will mention here just the awakening interest in the theory of rights, the recent attempts to ground the conclusions of Marxism in a methodology of rational choice, the surprising accommodation with once-despised pluralism, as well as the mounting enthusiasm for parliamentary forms. It used to be argued, for example, that the protection of the individual from other individuals and the state was a concern of a class-divided, exploitative society, in which individuals were indeed pitted against one another in a war of all against all. This mean-spirited version of the human condition would in time reveal itself for what it was, and such 'protections' would prove unnecessary in the world to which we should aspire. I am hard put to it to think of any Marxist or Marxist-influenced writer who would express such confidence today.

The history of Marxism warns against over-vaulting ambition and conveys an uncomfortable message to those who make too grandiose a claim. So while I believe that feminism, for its part, does revolutionize previous thinking, I think the success of that revolution can be hindered by arguments that go over the top. In relation to democracy, as in other crucial areas of contemporary politics, it is surely right to say that feminism introduces substantially new issues and dimensions, and this book will explore what these issues might be. But out of the range of ways in which feminism may transform the 'problems of democracy' – from identifying hitherto unspoken issues, to lending its weight to one side or another of already existing debates, to subverting the very principles and categories on which democracy has been thought to be based – I begin with no presumption in favour of any. Or perhaps I do. The meeting between feminist and democratic theory matters for both the prospective partners, and if the women's movement has some important lessons to pass on to the over-enthusiastic advocate of participatory democracy (see chapter 5), the conventions of democratic accountability also introduce some important elements into the debates over women's representation (see chapter 3). I do not see feminism as the final answer to questions that have been with us for centuries, and while this approach may infuriate in its apparent scepticism, the real insights of feminism should thereby emerge with greater force.

2

THE CLASSIC DEBATES

The starting point for modern theories of democracy is consent, for it was the idea that government is an artifice, legitimated only by the agreement of subjects who are 'naturally' free, that revived the democratic tradition. The notion took root in seventeenth-century Europe (to flower a hundred years later in the constitution of the USA) but was not at first described as democratic. Democracy, as C. B. Macpherson has observed, was 'a bad word' (1966: 1) and, with all its undesirable connotations, hardly a term that would strengthen one's case. For classical liberals, the problem was to explain how political authority could be justified even when citizens started out as naturally equal and free, and none of its early exponents (none too many of its later ones) dreamt that consent might be reinterpreted as votes for all. But the reference to choice and assent had its effect. Creaking open doors that had been shut for millenniums, it let what was to become liberal democracy make its unobtrusive entrance.

The last great moment of the democratic tradition lay far in the distant past. With a brief digression into the ideas of Machiavelli, David Held jumps a full two thousand years in his *Models of Democracy*, finding little of interest between the classical democracy of the Greek city-states and the birth of liberalism in seventeeth-century Europe. The Athenian ideals of civic participation (vitiated though they were by the exclusion of slaves, women and foreigners) sound extraordinary enough to our own ears, and were considered totally reprehensible by those who had heard of them three centuries ago. The citizens of Athens met at least forty times a year in their sovereign assembly (the quorum was 6,000) to debate and decide major issues of state. By a combination of voting and random selection, a more manageable council of 500 was chosen from among them to formulate policy proposals. Through a principle of rotation, its members then served on the committee of fifty; each president of this committee held office for only one day (Held 1986:23). The emphasis was on active participation and on each being ruled and ruler in turn. Citizens were expected to devote themselves to matters of general concern. Politics was no petty matter of protecting individual interest or concerns. The good citizen was he who transcended personal preoccupations to address the needs of the republic as a whole; the perfect citizen might not even perceive any conflict.

Nothing could be further from the 'protective democracy' that developed out of the liberal tradition. In the writings of Thomas Hobbes or John Locke, the private individual was prior: both theoretically in explaining how states come about, and politically in providing the touchstone for legitimate rule. Civil society was formed through a social contract. With a sharp eye to what most served their private interests, individuals came to see political order as necessary to let them get on with their lives; but it was this consent, and only this consent, that gave governments the right to rule. In the strident Hobbesian version, this had little to do with what we think of as democratic control, for 'consent' was still consent at the other end of a gun, and the sovereign needed absolute power. In the more restrained (and considerably more popular) version proposed by Locke, the responsibilities of government were finite, and individuals retained the right to overthrow a sovereign who had exceeded his legitimate role. Locke was no revolutionary and carefully reassured his readers that conservatism and inertia would delay any precipitate action for change. He further toned down the effect by accepting what he called 'tacit consent' as an adequate proof of agreement. Consent lacked substance in either case. For Hobbes, the agreement still stood even when extracted under fear of death; for Locke, the mere act of walking down a public highway, or of staying in the country rather than fleeing elsewhere, showed that you accepted society's rules. These were major and significant qualifications, yet with all this, a new note had definitely been sounded. The power of rulers was henceforth justified only by the consent of those who are ruled.

The individual had become the key to legitimate government –

but not of course just any old individual. Athenian democracy had restricted the rights and responsibilities of citizenship to a minority, and while having no truck with a property-based franchise, had excluded women, immigrants and slaves. John Locke spoke for all classical liberals in insisting on the property dimension. The 'individuals' whose consent mattered to theorists of the seventeenth and eighteenth centuries were men (sic) of property, and it was their interests that government had been created to serve. Those who were not even acknowledged as individuals were therefore doubly deprived, for they had no claim to democratic involvement and no (separate) interests they could insist on as their own. Children were out. Lunatics were out. So too were servants, who existed as appendages of their masters. So too were women, who were most definitively subsumed under men.

By the nineteenth century, the property qualification was being eroded and the franchise extended to cover a majority of men. The idea that workers were 'represented' by their employers had become a nonsense in the course of the industrial revolution, but the idea that women were represented by men retained its powerful hold. As anti-suffragists repeatedly asserted, women had no need of a voice of their own, for they had fathers and husbands to speak for their interests and it made no sense to think of women apart. (Feminists rightly identified the single woman living without either father or husband as the weak link in this chain. The thin-end-of-the-wedge tactic that led some to view the enfranchisement of single women as the priority proved a major source of tension in the women's movement, but it had a certain pragmatic appeal.)

Married women had least claim to the coveted status of 'individual', and until very late in the day the doctrine of coverture denied them a legal position. Once married, women became nonpersons. Outside of the aristocracy, which always retained its own rules, women could not hold property in their own name; they could not enter contracts or go to court on their own behalf; they had no rights against their husbands; they had no claims to custody over their children. In lengthy and hard-fought campaigns for reform, women insisted that they were individuals too, and that they should share with men those private rights over one's person, property and children, and should join with men in exercising public consent. Liberalism set the terms within which they had to make their case, and they drew on its traditions to apply consent to women as well.

In this context it made good sense to stress the individual as opposed to the couple, but the emphasis on the individual has usually been one of the points of departure for those who criticize the liberal tradition. The other is the determined separation liberals make between public and private spheres. Where liberalism produced a positive impulse rather than just a belated concession to democracy, this stemmed from a deeply felt imperative to protect citizens from those who rule. Democratic procedures were thought of in terms of limits to governmental power, linking the pursuit of democracy to its simultaneous circumscription. The power of government was to be contained by carefully delineating the boundaries within which it should operate; the private realm was to be freed from illegitimate interference of the state. The pressure for greater democracy in the public sphere (extending, for example, the categories of those who can vote) thus went hand in hand with pressure to restrict the spheres in which 'democracy' was relevant, producing the schizophrenia of which John Stuart Mill is the classic agonized example. Mill lent his support to campaigns to extend the suffrage – especially to women, but also to working-class men – yet lived in barely contained anxiety that governments who could then claim to 'represent' the people would think themselves entitled to almost infinite power. He offered his much-debated distinction between self-regarding and other-regarding activities as one means of thwarting this move, arguing that only the latter became legitimate affairs for the state. As subsequent critics have noted, the distinction is not up to the task. In the complex and interrelated world we inhabit, there is virtually no action performed by an individual which is without some impact on other people's lives. Does this mean governments can interfere in them all?

Anxiety is the essence of the liberal condition, the inseparable and (let me be sexist) the nagging companion of that seemingly boundless confidence with which liberal philosophers transformed their world. Liberalism emerged out of an empiricist philosophy which took experience as the source of all knowledge and abandoned previous beliefs in innate ideas. This was to prove immensely exciting for the natural sciences, but for political theorists it had more dubious effect. When the individual stepped on to the stage as the source of all knowledge and fount of all meaning, he walked into a scenario calculated to produce maximum despair. No truth beyond what we can work out with our own endowment of reason; no shared experience beyond an equal fear of each other; no common interests save those our reason may reveal. With appropriate modesty, John Locke described himself as a mere 'underlabourer', and as Sheldon Wolin argues, he 'confined man to a middling sort of condition, incapable of omniscience or perfection, "a state of mediocrity, which is not capable of extremes"' (1960:296–7). The human mind was felt to be a feeble tool for achieving final knowledge of the world. For the best of us, it could produce only tentative results. The vast majority would do well to abide by the teachings of the church. Wolin notes that Locke frequently referred to a project of reducing ethics to a set of clearly demonstrable mathematical propositions, but never delivered on this promise. It is probable that 'he was deterred by the limited social utility of the idea. The bulk of mankind would not have been able to comprehend the work' (p. 336). The very ambition of empiricist philosophy brought with it a loss of certainty – reinforcing the anxiety of the liberal condition.

Small wonder that Sheldon Wolin describes liberalism as 'a philosophy of sobriety, born in fear, nourished by disenchantment, and prone to believe that the human condition was and was likely to remain one of pain and anxiety' (pp. 293–4); or that Benjamin Barber sums up the liberal psychology as one in which 'we are born into the world solitary strangers, live our lives as wary aliens, and die in fearful isolation' (1984:68). Driven by private needs and interests, seeing in others only a threatening mirror of themselves, the individuals of the classic tradition were in desperate need of protection. The most radically individualist of seventeenth-century thinkers was not as a result what we would call liberal at all. Thomas Hobbes saw no solution beyond total abnegation, for life was only possible under a regime of absolute power.

Radical individualism sees the individual as prior to society, and hardly acknowledges that society exists at all. In its more extreme versions, this is no longer in tune with the mood of our time. The idea that the individual is a 'social individual', bound up in a network of social relations, is more consistently the orthodoxy of today. There are occasional lapses: Margaret Thatcher declared in 1987 that there is no such thing as society, but she quickly covered her tracks. The real problems in grounding a theory of democracy on liberal individualism lie not so much in its peculiar sociology (though this is peculiar indeed) as in the impoverished notions of what politics and consent are about. The scope of politics is carefully bounded, while consent is emptied of real content. Even when grudgingly extended to include all adults (or at least all who are 'nationals', for very many still live under a government whose composition they cannot affect), universal suffrage offers the formality of acquiescence as its measure of popular choice. We can 'choose' whether to vote or abstain, but whichever we do are equally bound by results. We can 'choose' between competing parties, but cannot expect to control what these parties will decide to do. The impact of each individual's choice is so minimal that political theorists have had to say that it is irrational to go out and vote, for the chances of any one of us swaying the final outcome are so slender that it is extraordinary we bother at all. 'The true ideal of majority rule', as Philip Green puts it, 'is not that everyone has equal influence, but that no one has any influence!' (1985a: 171).

Where consent is nonetheless regarded as crucial to liberalism's democratic pretensions, it is sometimes reworked in what Carole Pateman (1979) has described as a 'hypothetical voluntarism': modern-day versions of John Locke's tacit consent, in which our still being here is taken as evidence that we agree. But more often that not, liberal democracy rests its claims on having set clear limits to what governments can do. Our societies are said to be democratic not so much because they have developed mechanisms through which we can explicitly and significantly register our consent, as because they work within the boundaries of individual right. A democratic government is one that accepts and defends free speech, freedom of publication and freedom of association. Obedience to these rules is what keeps it democratic.

Public and private realms I have noted that critics of liberalism home in on its separation between public and private realms, and query its image of the individual. On the first point, socialists have long argued that the liberal distinction between public and private erects a facade of political equality over a society teeming with the grossest inequalities, seeing this juxtaposition of democracy in one sphere with subordination in the other as liberalism's decisive failure. The notional boundary between public and private has been equally central to feminist analysis, but the emphasis is different. First, feminists have noted that liberalism is not the only tradition to erect such boundaries, for some version of this distinction has influenced every political thinker and every period of political life. 'Distinctions between public and private have been and remain fundamental, not incidental or tangential, ordering principles in all known societies save, perhaps, the most simple' (Elshtain 1981:6). For Plato and Aristotle the public world of politics was counterposed to the private world of the household, the latter being at this point the sphere both of production and reproduction. The household was necessary but all too mundane and could not nourish the kind of rationality, wisdom, indeed heroism, which the polity would rightly demand (Okin 1979; Elshtain 1981:ch.1). For Aristotle, this meant women had no place in politics, for their 'nature' was such that it fitted them only for the inferior virtues of the private sphere. Plato, unusually, considered women as possible candidates for the highest political role, but his *Republic* required the elite Guardians to forgo private homes, sexual or family attachments. Even as he seemed to challenge it, he firmly reinstated the convention that the preoccupations of household and family are incompatible with public life.

Liberalism recast the boundaries between public and private, but in doing so it made not one but two distinctions. This is the second major point feminists have made, in an argument that echoes some of Hannah Arendt's thesis in *The Human Condition* (1958). Arendt noted that in the ancient world there was simply one division – between the exposed public world of the *polis* and the hidden private world of the household. The household was in those days both family and economy but, with the subsequent separation of these two, the new category of the social emerged 'from the shadowy interior of the household into the light of the public sphere' (p. 38). This changed the meaning and significance of the public/private divide. The social began to do battle with the political as to which was to reign supreme, and from Arendt's point of view, won a depressing victory. Politics became the handmaiden of social interest, while the residual household sphere found itself threatened on every side. Privacy in the ancient world was literally a state of privation, from which citizens desired escape. In our own era it has become something to be defended against the erosions of political and social life.

Hannah Arendt draws no feminist conclusions from this, but her richer appreciation of (at least) three terms – the private/household, the public/social, the public/political – is reflected in current feminist thought. Carole Pateman, in particular, has argued that liberal theory provides us with a 'double separation'. Domestic life was initially seen as the most irreduceably private, something distinguished in its essential principles from all of civil society, which in this context then appeared as the 'public' domain. The familial was not in fact ignored in classical theory (in Hobbes or Locke, for example, we find explicit discussions of the power of husbands over wives and the power of parents over children) but once the social contract had been theorized, the domestic dropped all too rapidly from view. The creation of civil society came to be seen as the creation of consenting *men*, and it was the relationship between this (male) society and its (male) government that then preoccupied liberal thought. Subsequent battles between liberals and socialists centred on the divisions between public and private, political and social, state and market. But 'because liberalism conceptualises civil society in abstraction from ascriptive domestic life, the latter remains "forgotten" in theoretical discussion. The separation between private and public is thus re-established as a division *within* civil society itself, within the world of men' (Pateman 1983:285).

We can see the importance of this if we look at writers like Rousseau, who combines an argument over the interdependence of political and social equality with a determined exclusion of women from political life. In one version of the public/private divide he appears as a radical critic, condemning the notion that what goes on in the 'private' sphere of property relations is irrelevant to political debate. But in the other sense of the 'private', he is foremost among those who associated women with the lesser virtues of love and affection, regarding them as 'naturally' unsuited to the demands of justice, and best kept safely at home. A century later, that best of liberals, John Stuart Mill, also began to edge towards challenging the first distinction between public and private when he suggested that political participation was learnt in civil society and that workers as well as employers needed to develop their capacities for decision-making and judgement in the regulation of their working lives. But while he argued additionally for the enfranchisement of women, he saw no contradiction in anticipating that the majority of women would continue to 'choose' the career of motherhood and home. In the second distinction between public and private, he remained an orthodox. He seemed not to notice that women would then be confined to the domestic domain and hence immunized from that learning process he had presented as so important.

For feminists, the failure to explore the nature of the (most) private sphere is a failure in democratic debate. Women and men are not equally autonomous and free, and just as socialists have stressed the way that class inequalities subvert supposed political equality, so feminists have stressed the way that inequalities in marriage and the household make a nonsense of equal political rights. The practical implications can seem somewhat bathetic: the need, for example, for improved provision of nurseries in order to equalize access to political life. But much of the argument has been more conceptually challenging, suggesting that the liberal distinctions between public and private secure a version of the individual that remains resolutely male. For Carole Pateman, for example, the exclusion of the domestic from the realm of civil society creates a 'private' individual who is abstracted from familial relations, and it is largely because of this that he can venture forth into the political arena as the classically liberal owner of property in his person. C. B. Macpherson has introduced into our language the notion of the 'possessive individual' as the cornerstone of liberal thought. From feminist perspectives, this liberal individual is male, and his proprietorial character owes as much to his relation to women as to anything that capitalism could invent. A more richly textured notion of the relationship between public and private thus gives us new insight into the abstractions of liberal individualism. It is no accident that women were so long excluded from those who consent; it may indeed prove intrinsic to liberal democracy that it cannot acknowledge women as citizens in the fullest sense of the word.

The individual is not gender-neutral C. B. Macpherson has argued that the individual of liberal theory is a historically specific one. The market society of seventeenth-century Europe generated a notion of man as appropriator, defined by what he owned – which included himself as well as possessions – and motivated by the desire for more. Freedom was then retheorized as not having to depend on others; with the development of the market, freedom became a function of possessions. The difference between the wage worker and the slave was that the former 'freely' entered into a contract to allow others the use of his capacity for work. Unlike the slave the wage worker owned his person and capacities; he was a proprietor on however small a scale. For Macpherson this is not just a trick but an unfortunate truth. 'The individual in market society *is* human as proprietor of his own person. However much he may wish it to be otherwise, his humanity does depend on his freedom from any but self-interested contractual relations with others' (Macpherson 1962:275). The difference between one proprietor and another – between employer and worker, landlord and tenant – is then submerged in the underlying unity that all are proprietors of themselves. Macpherson sought to translate these possessive individuals into active creators, free to use and develop their powers. But because he focused exclusively on the way that the market relations of civil society have formed (or deformed) our notions of human development, he had nothing to say about changes in the domestic zone. Democracy (public) is currently constrained by the market (private); its potential will only be realized by changing market relations.

Benjamin Barber likewise sees liberalism as dependent on a specific notion of the individual, though in his case there is little curiosity as to the material developments that might be necessary to bring about change. The individuals of liberal theory have been conceptualized as at the mercy of their needs and interests, and it is the conflicts that potentially rage between them that then define what democracy must do. Liberal democracy is, he suggests, 'politics as zookeeping':

> From the perspective of this political zoology, civil society is an alternative to the 'jungle' – to the war of all against all that defines the state of nature. In that poor and brutish war, the beasts howl in voices made articulate by reason – for zoos, for cages and trainers, for rules and regulations, for regular feeding times and prudent custodians. Like captured leopards, men are to be admired for their proud individuality and for their unshackled freedom, but they must be caged for their untrustworthiness and antisocial orneriness all the same. Indeed if the individual is dangerous, the species is deadly. Liberal democracy's sturdiest cages are reserved for the People. (1984:20–1)

Unlike Macpherson, Barber offers no analysis of the social or economic foundations which produced this version of the human individual, and his argument is weakened by his seeming confidence that we can just substitute an alternative view. But note again the reference to an undifferentiated 'civil society'. Including the domestic domain? Excluding the domestic domain? Even if we pass over in tolerant silence the unreconstructed reference to men, his argument stresses the peculiarity of the liberal individual, but does not enquire whether his content might be explicitly male.

To add one final light from the male firmament, Charles Taylor argues in his critical essay on 'Atomism' that any theory which rests on the individual is making a claim with substance about what being an individual implies. In particular, the idea that human beings have rights, but not so – or less so – animals, trees, rocks and mountains, must rest on a notion of the specifically human capacities that command our respect. It is not just anything that makes human beings different from animals that is thought to justify our rights: 'most animals cannot scratch themselves in the small of their backs, but this does not induce us to inscribe this capacity in the UN Charter' (1985:193). There are certain characteristically human capacities, of which he suggests that the ability to make choices is one of the most fundamental, which we regard as worthy, and it is on the basis of these that we develop our notions of rights. If this is so, it is surely incoherent to ascribe rights to men (Taylor always talks of men) because of certain worthy capacities, yet claims to be indifferent over what kind of society best nurtures and develops them. 'The doctrine of the primacy of rights is not as independent as its proponents want to claim from considerations about human nature and the human social condition' (p. 197). The 'individual' in whose name we claim these rights has content, and the content is more than just being alive.

Taylor makes this point in order to show that the language of rights is not an alternative to arguments about the good society, and that rights of themselves lead on to more substantial issues about the kind of society we need. Untouched as he is by feminist debate, he does not explore the further possibility that the content we give to human identity is gendered, but his argument lends unknowing support to the case made by feminists. If the individual is stripped of all substance, then it cannot carry the weight it has shouldered in political theory. When it does have substance, masculinity and femininity creep in. Whatever candidates we might offer for specifically human identity – rationality, autonomy, ability to make choices – they all turn out to have a sexual history. The very ideal of reason, which might seem if anything does to stand above sex, has been formulated and reformulated in a series of dichotomies between higher and lower, mind and body, reason and passion, in which the best parts were always claimed by the male (Lloyd 1984). For contemporary feminists, the individual is highly suspect. Behind his supposedly gender-free guise, he remains unmistakeably a man.

The crucial building blocks of liberal democracy are the individual, citizenship, rights and consent, and it has been argued by a growing number of feminists that these categories are themselves male. The argument is most thoroughly associated with the work of Carole Pateman, and though its development can be traced through her writings over the last decade (see the invaluable collection, Pateman 1989) it has its clearest exposition in *The Sexual Contract*. The democracy of liberal democracy is centred, as we have already seen, around the paradigmatic notion of contract. Free individuals enter voluntarily into agreements – contracts – which involve them giving up some things in exchange for others. A democratic society cannot be premised on forced submission (obey me, or else I'll be round with my gun); nor can it be based on ascribed roles (I was born to rule and you to obey). But nor is it based, in the liberal democratic tradition, on any substantial activities of participation or consent. The claim to democracy stands or falls by its notion of *voluntary* submission: we agree to be ruled because we get something – political order, protection of rights, including now the right to vote – in return. Pateman's argument is that it is impossible to incorporate women into this framework in anything but the most ambiguous and uncertain of ways. Women thus serve as the definitive argument against liberal democracy.

Part of her argument is historical. If we examine the foundations of liberalism we can see that it was no 'accidental' oversight that excluded women from the original social contract, but that this was central to what the contract entailed. Men, she argues, sought a new consensual basis for political order which would challenge previous notions that the rulers had the 'right' to rule. But they also wanted to overthrow the 'rule of the fathers' in another sense, establishing a fraternity in which the brothers were assured access to the bodies of women. No longer at the mercy of the patriarch's whims, which up till then had granted or withheld the right to marry as a 'gift' from fathers to sons, men could now establish their own direct paths of access in what was to become an increasingly formalized marriage contract. The contract was between husband and wife (the fathers were pushed out of the picture) but it was an entirely one-sided contract in which the women gave obedience in return for protection. And while subsequent campaigns have modified the nature of the contract, establishing some independent rights for wives over their incomes or custody of their children, there is one profoundly important respect in which the marriage contract still denies wives a right of resistance. With few exceptions, contemporary legislation does not yet acknowledge the existence of marital rape. As long as a woman is a wife, she has no 'right' to refuse sex to her man.

The political status of women, Carole Pateman argues, is bound up with this. The contract between husband and wife served for two and a half centuries as the basis on which women were denied the status of individuals – and were not thus privy to the social contract, or the later strengthening of democratic control. History has since moved on and women have won the right to vote and even to become political leaders themselves, but their status as individuals remains uncertain and ambiguous. According to Pateman, the individual of liberal theory has written into it a notion of sexual mastery, of individuals as possessing themselves, and wanting and needing to possess others. 'The "individual" is a patriarchal category. The individual is masculine and his sexuality is understood accordingly (1988:184–5). The identity between freedom and possession, and the associated equation between consent and subordination, is not then just a product of market relations, but depends on something more. Marxists have argued that the problem with the employment contract is that workers contract out their labour power in an 'agreement' that then gives employers absolute power to do with it whatever they will. If we look beyond this to the marriage contract, the prostitution contract or, drawing on most recent developments, the surrogate mother-hood contract, we can identify more clearly what is wrong. In these latter contracts, the body of the woman is not incidental, for it is only because she is a woman that she is sought after for this kind of deal. What sort of (free) agreement is it that hands over the use of one's body to another? that treats our bodies as possessions that can be alienated to somebody else? The notions of consent and freedom that underlie liberal philosophy are grounded in the experience of the male.

The clincher, in a number of Carole Pateman's arguments, is the issue of rape. Rape trials confirm that women's consent is not yet regarded in the same light as men's, for with all the increased publicity around rape trials and supposedly heightened aware-ness of feminist issues, judges continue to comment that a woman's 'no' means 'yes', and proving that she said 'no' is not enough to win a conviction. The woman's word has to be independently confirmed by the more reliable evidence of physi-cal brutality; and even when the court accepts that she did not consent, the man can legitimately claim he misunderstood. What does this tell us about women and consent? For Carole Pateman, 'the identification of enforced submission with consent in rape is a stark example of the wider failure in liberal democratic theory and practice to distinguish free commitment and agreement by equals from domination, subordination and inequality' (1980:162). The experience of women reveals in all its depressing characteristics the perversity of liberal democracy. As far as voting is concerned, women were at first denied even the chance to say 'yes' or 'no'. Then they got on to the electoral roll, but this did not solve the problem. Within the parameters of liberal democracy, consent has been understood in a way that deprives it of meaning. In the world of the law courts, women's consent will be assumed even in the face of explicit denial; in the world of politics, we may have voted for another party, but by virtue of voting are said to give our consent to whatever is the result. In the world of the law courts, our consent still stands though it leads directly to domination; in the world of politics, we elected these governments and cannot complain if they abolish our rights.

In tune with much recent feminist writing, Pateman has reclaimed the body as a central concern. Identity does not float freely through the abstractions of consciousness. It is embodied in some physical form. Liberalism has clung resolutely to the abstractions of its individual, and not just to absolve itself from responsibility for social concerns: 'abstraction from the body is also necessary if the "individual" is not to be revealed as a masculine figure' (1989:4). The 'man' cannot represent both women and men, for the bodily differences between us do indeed matter. If we continue to pretend that the individual is abstract and disembodied, we will be silently accepting his masculine shape. The alternative is to abandon the search for a better abstraction, and admit there are women and men. 'To take embodied identity seriously demands the abandonment of the masculine unitary individual to open up space for two figures; one masculine, one feminine' (1988:224).

The argument is deeply shocking to admirers of abstract thought, and its precise implications in terms of how we should view democracy have remained teasingly vague. But to give it additional weight, think of the more accessible issue of sexual equality, where the arguments against the abstract individual are perhaps clearer. In *The Female Body and the Law* (1989), Zillah Eisenstein takes up what has been an acute problem for feminists seeking redress through the law. Should we be stressing equality or difference? Is the problem that the law continues to discriminate between women and men? Or that it fails to do so? Should we be calling for an end to legislation that differentiates between the sexes: that prevents women from playing an equal role in combat forces, or, in the case of Britain, from work in the mines? Or should we be calling for more sex-specific legislation that will acknowledge and meet women's different needs: employment rights for pregnant women, for example, which the USA (alone among wealthy industrialized countries) does not yet have? Strict equality legislation may abstract from the real conditions of women, giving them the formality of equal opportunity, but in practice leaving them stuck in a subordinate role. The alternative, however, is a risky business, for sex-specific legislation writes into our laws and practices that women are 'naturally' different from men – which may confirm men as normal and ourselves in need of special help.

For Eisenstein, the dilemma rests on the abstractions of the individual. The male has been the reference point in all our phallocratic discourses, with the supposedly gender-free language of individuals an increasingly threadbare disguise. In terms reminiscent of Carole Pateman's analysis, she argues that 'the individual is a man, in a man's body' (Eisenstein 1989:77). Our discussions of sexual equality have always silently privileged this male body. When men and women are treated the same, it means women are treated as if they were men; when men and women are treated differently, the man is the norm, against which the woman is peculiar, lacking and different. Feminism has been endlessly locked into this equality/difference dichotomy – they are the only choices on offer and yet neither will do. The alternative offered by Zillah Eisenstein is to 'pluralize the meaning of difference and reinvent the category of equality' (p. 4). Instead of *the* difference between male and female we need to recognize the many differences between women, between men, as well as between the two sexes. The pregnant woman is of course different from the never-pregnant man, but she is also different from the non-pregnant woman, and there are many variations even among those women who are pregnant. Allowing woman to be subsumed under the category of mother is as bad in its way as claiming she is the 'same' as man; both alternatives reflect an impoverished 'either/or' choice that limits our notions of equality. What we need, argues Eisenstein, is 'a radical sex/gender pluralism that will reconstitute the meaning of equality' (p. 199).

In the context of economic and social equality, this critique of false abstraction seems highly pertinent and helps resolve unnecessary dilemmas that arise from an abstract norm. The problem is how far we want to go. The feminist challenge to supposedly universal concepts has gathered remarkable speed over recent years and there are few candidates within the usual armoury of political theorists that have escaped critical attention. Citizenship, the individual, equality, freedom, rights: all these have been exposed to attack in arguments that detect not just gender bias, but gender itself in the list. This distinction matters, for whereas bias can be eliminated, gender *per se* will stick. Feminists have now shifted from criticizing misogyny and bias towards criticizing more fundamental assumptions; from saying that the content of current theories is oppressive to women, to challenging the proclaimed neutrality of the framework itself (Gatens 1986). If this more ambitious argument is right, then the problems of the liberal democratic individual are intrinsic to the concept. No amount of cleaning and dusting will make it suitable for use.

Participatory democracy The division between those who deal in the universalities and abstractions of the individual or the citizen and those who stress sexual difference is the major theoretical issue for feminist political theory today. In the less gender-specific formulations of universality versus particularity or foundationalism versus contingency (Rorty 1989), it is arguably the major theoretical issue within political theory itself. As far as this chapter is concerned, it arises explicitly in the feminist critiques of liberal and republican democracy, and implicitly in the discussion of participatory democracy. Because of this I shall postpone fuller discussion till I have outlined the other two models. For the moment, let me turn to the next major tradition: participatory democracy.

The distinctions between public and private spheres is one of the central points of debate in the arguments for a more participatory democracy. Supporters of this school argue that democratic government is subverted and denied by the blatantly undemocratic ways in which our social (usually working) lives are organized, and that a more substantial democracy will depend on restructuring the workplace to permit genuine and equal participation. Political equality is in other words inconsistent with social arrangements that deprive most of us of the chance to make decisions. Liberal versions of democracy do not begin to tackle the power structures that dictate our lives; it is a nonsense to concede universal suffrage for deciding who governs, yet leave vital decisions over employment, housing or education in non-elected hands. Liberalism has chosen to exclude huge areas of our existence from the procedures of democratic control, and with its well-worn distinctions between public and private has actively sustained an unequal distribution of power. Political equality becomes meaningless when it is restricted in this way.

The other aspect to this argument is developmental. Democratic practices are learnt in the supposedly 'private' world of family, school and work; because of this, it is absurd to espouse democracy at the level of the state when there is subordination in our lives elsewhere. In her other persona as the leading contemporary theorist of participatory democracy, Carole Pateman, for example, argues that 'the theory of participatory democracy stands or falls on two hypotheses: the educative function of participation, and the crucial role of industry' (1970:44). Drawing on empirical evidence from Gabriel Almond and Sidney Verba's comparative study of *The Civic Culture* (1963), she notes the high correlation between how much we participate in politics and whether we think of ourselves as competent or politically effective; and stresses the very clear indication that those who work under hierarchical control, with decisions taken over their heads, will attach least weight to political involvement. If we have no experience of affecting decisions at work, then we believe (with good reason) that there is nothing much we can do. The private sphere of work underpins the public world of politics; what happens in the one shapes and constrains what is likely to occur in the other.

The correlation between political participation and socioeconomic status has been exhaustively and depressingly established; though the supposed corollary which highlights our experience of control or participation at work is more widely contested. For example, in their somewhat odd investigation into the relationship between participation and class (odd in that it tries to isolate 'class' from all the things that have given it meaning), George Moyser and Geraint Parry (1987) claim that position in the occupational structure proves virtually insignificant and that the more striking correlations are with individual resources in terms of wealth and education, and with organizational ties in terms of membership of groups, parties or unions. The implication is that it does not much matter whether we experience work as autonomy or as subordination, for increased levels and possibilities of participation at work may have limited consequences for increased participation outside. Democracy in one sphere may have little or no consequences for democracy in the other. The argument can be qualified to cope with this, as Robert Dahl (a recent and perhaps surprising recruit to the cause of economic democracy) has shown. He remains agnostic over the relationship between greater participation in workplace decisions and greater activity as citizens, but argues that the case for the first still stands even if it has no effect at all on the second. If democracy is supposed to be justified in governing a state, then it is equally justified in a firm (Dahl 1985:41). Whatever principles are deemed desirable in the public sphere of politics, they are surely of equal worth in the private economic sphere.

As well as calling into question the public/private divide, the participatory model has usually stressed the value of the meeting above the anonymity of the vote, calling for more direct involvement in political decisions. This is one of the points at which the contrast of liberal versus participatory democracy overlaps with that of representative versus direct, though there is in fact no necessary link between the two (Mansbridge 1980; Bobbio 1984). In Britain, for example, activists in trade unions and the Labour Party have traditionally argued for the meeting as the way to make decisions, for in the meeting we get the stories behind all the issues and have to grapple with the arguments on each side. The usual alternative of postal ballots reduces this to a cross on a form in the privacy of the home, leaving judgements based on undigested bias, and giving the media undue influence on results. Advocates of participatory democracy usually query the privacy, anonymity and passivity of this kind of 'involvement'.

The same emphasis on direct face-to-face involvement surfaces in a preference for the binding mandate, which until recently was taken as one of the hallmarks of the radical approach (see Bobbio 1984). The scale of contemporary society inevitably forces us to rely on representation, for we cannot hope to meet together in citizens' assemblies and take all decisions ourselves. We can however minimize the effects of size by binding our representatives to pre-agreed policies and programmes. Thus instead of electing them to do what they think to be best, we can keep them still accountable to the meeting. The British Labour Party again serves as an example, though in a substantially modified form. In the 1970s, there was a successful campaign to introduce the reselection of councillors and MPs, so that instead of being 'chosen' to represent a constituency for life, they had to defend their record during each term of office, and could not assume they would be selected next time.

The binding mandate has not featured strongly in feminist theory or practice, and indeed I shall argue in later chapters that feminism has evaded important issues of accountability. In other ways, however, the feminist and participatory traditions have been intimately connected. The contemporary women's movement has been almost an experiment in participatory democracy, with a politics of grass-roots activism, a radical critique of authority and a commitment to collective decisions. As such it deserves a chapter to itself. More theoretically, the feminist focus on divisions between public and private has made the question of *where* democracy should be practised a central, inescapable concern. This, too, is discussed more fully later on. Most significantly at this stage, the feminist critique of the abstract individual lends itself to a politics of participation and talk. Diversity, difference, differences, seem to be emerging as central preoccupations in a feminist perspective on democracy. If this is so, they point to active discussion and participation as the key.

Liberal democracy sets up voting as the main, or even only, mechanism through which we can voice our needs and interests. Yet voting can leave us in isolation; it does not allow for texture or nuance and does not create space for transformation or change. One of the defining characteristics of contemporary feminism has been its emphasis on the ways in which women get trapped into a culture of passivity and self-denial. One of the most direct conclusions from this is that women have to 'learn' what they want, learn to challenge the silent privileging of the male. In this sense, the emphasis that the women's movement has placed on consciousness-raising (despite the unfortunate overtones of a consciousness that starts out too low) reflects in practice what writers like Carole Pateman and Zillah Eisenstein have argued in their theoretical work. The language through which we think our needs, interests or rights continually subverts the impulse to liberation, drawing us back into the either/or dichotomies of being like men, or else 'naturally' different; it holds out the illusions of a gender-free equality, and then stamps it firmly on the head. Women themselves are as much at the mercy of these dichotomies as men; it is not just that we 'know' what we want but have been unable to make ourselves heard. Voting *per se* cannot deal with this, for it is changing our perceptions and agendas that is the more urgent and difficult task. For reasons such as these, most feminists have come to regard discussion, talk and active participation as vital, and to this extent allied themselves to the participatory camp. Feminists have also, however, had their criticisms, focusing on the priority participatory democracy gives to work-place involvement, and the way this continues to privilege the male.

Problems of participation The conventional responses to the participatory model come in two forms: those horrified – incensed – by its notion of democracy; and those sympathetic but reluctantly opposed. A good example from the first camp is Giovanni Sartori, who has for many years represented the 'minimalist' school of democracy and whose *Theory of Democracy Revisited* (1987) makes a number of telling points. The most important of these deals with the problem of numerical equality. Periodic elections may look inadequate when measured against classic ideals (Sartori asks us to clear these ridiculous ideals from our head) but they do at least provide a way in which all of the people can make themselves heard. 'If democracy grants – as it does – the right to decide their destiny to *all* the people, then the opinions that indicate a general consensus or, conversely, a generalized dissensus about governing are the opinions delivered by the voters at large at elections and via elections only' (p. 89). Supporters of direct or participatory democracy are always agitating for more active involvement, but their alternatives are usually seized on by a vocal minority, who cannot be trusted to represent us all.

More participation (workplace meetings, direct action, demonstrations) can end up denying the majority their voice. More 'democracy' will therefore lead to more elitism, in which 'the few do better and count for more, than the passive, inert, apathetic, nonparticipant many' (Sartori 1987:114). This model of democracy 'covers up, under a fashionable and most convenient disguise, the displacement by counter-elites of pre-existing elites' (p. 116); and Sartori warns that these new elites will prove much worse than the old. Those who participate are by definition those who take their politics seriously; and in a sleight of hand only partially justified by reference to empirical work (p. 118), Sartori correlates intensity with extremism and intolerance, with a refusal to acknowledge counter-argument or to deal with embarrassing facts. The democracy of periodic elections may not give individuals much scope for exerting control, but it does at least guarantee the moderate and the passive their say.

There *is* a sleight of hand here. Even if those who get involved in political parties or movements are more likely to occupy clearly defined positions on the political spectrum, this does not mean they will be more intolerant or more dangerously 'intense'. It could equally well be argued that continuous involvement in meetings and decision-making improves our understanding of the complexities of political choice; that it reduces intolerance and narrow self-interest and makes us listen more generously to what others have to say. This is a key point put forward by Benjamin Barber.

But if the case against more active involvement is not proven on one side, neither is it proven on the other. New Left politics had barely got into its stride when Michael Walzer wrote his 'Day in the life of a socialist citizen' (1970), pointing out the terrible pressures participation puts on people's time. Though infinitely more sympathetic to the ideals than Sartori, he, too, speaks 'for the irresponsible non-participant', 'the part-time activist, the half-virtuous man' (p. 234), and notes that not everyone wants to go to meetings all the time. People want to get on with their private lives as well – to 'take long walks, play with their children, paint pictures, make love, and watch television' – and the 'community people' who attend all the meetings will barely see their children at all. It is a mark of the time (this was only 1970) that Walzer can make the latter point without seeming to notice that it affects women more than men, but the power of the argument remains. The life of an active citizen would leave little margin for anything else, and this being so, is it really what we want?

Some people find it hard enough even to get out for the four-yearly ritual. What would happen if they were called on to be more active still, to participate in the workplace meeting, the citizens' assembly, the neighbourhood forum and so on? The numbers involved would inevitably be low, and while it is logically possible that the range of views represented by those who turned up would coincide exactly with the range in the electorate as a whole, there is no guarantee that this would occur. This is the point stressed by Jane Mansbridge (1980). Despite her initial enthusiasm for participatory democracy, she concludes that democracy requires proportionate outcomes and that as long as a society contains different interests and views, these need to be adequately – that is, proportionately – reflected. It may well be a problem with the vote that it ignores ambiguities in whether we really 'know' our interests and views. But the problem with the meeting is that so many of us are too busy to go.

The onslaught on the participatory school has had remarkable success in recent years and the confident optimism of the 1960s or

1970s has very substantially eroded. Among British radicals, for example, the meeting has fallen into disrepute as the preserve of an unrepresentative few; and in a range of debates over proportional representation or the use of postal ballots for trade union and party decisions, the liberal democratic emphasis on the vote has substantially replaced the participatory emphasis on the meeting. In the course of the 1980s the Conservative Government introduced industrial relations legislation that forced unions to ballot all members before embarking on 'legal' strikes. This was undoubtedly conceived as a means of reducing trade union militancy by giving the moderates more weight, and was initially condemned by radicals as such. But it did not take long for the awkwardness of this response to sink in and there are few radicals who would now object to the principle of one person, one vote.

From feminist perspectives, two key problems with participatory democracy are its failure to recognize the additional burdens on women's time, and its emphasis on the workplace as the most important site of increased participation. If men have trouble getting round to all of those meetings, then what about the democratic woman? Every society I know defines women as the carers: those ultimately responsible for looking after the old, the young and the sick, not to mention their able-bodied husbands. Where the social provision is good, women still carry greater responsibility than men; where (as more often) the social provision is poor, the hours of the day are consumed by their jobs, their children, their homes. The fact that some of this 'work' is a pleasure is not particularly to the point, for whether people enjoy it or not, it nonetheless has to be done. The available time left over for meetings will not amount to much, and a day in the life of a socialist citizeness will not be sustainable for long.

The other central complaint relates to the importance attached to paid work. It is part of the way I have defined participatory democracy that economic or industrial democracy plays a major role in its vision of the future, for anyone who criticizes the minimalism of liberal democracy and yet shows no interest in the workplace will fit more neatly into my 'republican' camp. Participationists proper reject the conventional distinction between public and private spheres and seek to extend the scope of democracy by embracing worker self-management, worker co-operatives, democratic decision-making at work. In doing so, however, they reflect a perennial masculine bias. Most men will hope to work full-time through the majority of their adult years and will see their identities as bound up with their working role. For many of them, the work environment will represent their harshest experience of authority, and a thoroughgoing democratization of the workplace will very substantially enhance the degree to which they can exert control. Most women, by contrast, have a more broken and distanced relationship to their place of work. Even with the extraordinary increase in female wage employment since the Second World War, women have to take time off work to have babies, frequently return to employment on a part-time basis and almost invariably have to juggle their time between their paid and unpaid employment. In recent decades, the workplace has become considerably more significant in defining and directing women's lives, but women's relationship to work remains profoundly different from men's. They may experience their harshest subordination not at work but at home, while the time they can devote to worker self-management will be severely constrained.

Liberal theorists may have written men into their notion of the individual, but supporters of participatory democracy stand accused of an even more direct discrimination. The individual can at least pretend to be sexually neutral, but no one who gives it a moment of thought would say the same is true about work. Men and women have a different relationship to work, and a different relationship to time, and no version of democracy that rests its case on increased participation at work can be neutral between women and men. As Carole Pateman notes, the debate between liberal and radical democrats has revolved endlessly around one particular notion of public and private, concentrating on 'whether the economy and workplace are private or public and whether democracy in the workplace is feasible or desirable' (1989:5). Neither of the opposing positions deals with women's lives.

With all this, there is still an alliance of sorts between contemporary feminism and participatory democracy, based on their common disquiet with the public/private distinction and cemented by their enthusiasm for discussion and talk. The disagreements begin with the different meanings they attach to the public and private spheres, and yet in comparison with the last of my three models, this divergence might not seem so great. Feminists share a good deal with the supporters of participatory democracy; with those who represent the tradition of civic republicanism, they might seem to share nothing at all. As Hannah Pitkin observes, theorists of this last school seem to appeal specifically to patriarchal values and have often set up the 'feminine' as the realm from which real politics must escape. 'From the political ideals of ancient Athens to their recent revival by Hannah Arendt, republican activism seems to be linked to "manly" heroism and military glory, and to disdain for the household, the private, the personal, and the sensual. Is this a fortuitous or a significant linkage, and how is it to be understood?' (Pitkin 1984:5).

Civic republicanism The history of republicanism stretches back far beyond the liberal tradition, and writers like Pocock (1975) have shown how ideals of the classical Greek republic were revived in Renaissance Italy, and then carried through again into the values of the American revolution. In its historical antecedents, this tradition is ominously dismissive of femininity and women. Aristotle, for example, saw only men as political animals and thought women were fashioned by nature for the necessities of household affairs; and 'nothing is more striking in Machiavelli's explicit remarks on women than his contempt for the "weaker sex"' (Pitkin 1984:109). As revived in twentieth-century (and mostly North-American) debates, the crucial elements of republicanism are the notion of politics as a very special kind of activity that sets human beings apart; the idea that being a citizen means transcending the particular interests of the individual or group; and the emphasis on activity and participation as what makes a democracy real. As a critique of liberal orthodoxy, the republican tradition therefore shares certain preoccupations with the participatory school, but registers a more profound distaste for the kind of huckstering politics in which everything becomes a matter of individual interest or gain. The two traditions diverge decisively over the distinction between public and private spheres. One queries the pertinence of the distinction, arguing that democratic principles should be applied equally throughout both spheres; the other wants to reassert a specifically political sphere.

Hannah Arendt is one of the most powerful figures in this tradition, though her originality means she fits uneasily into any school or camp. Looking back to the age of the Greek city-states, she contrasts their notion of public responsibility with the modern subordination of politics to private gain. True politics, she insists, 'is never for the sake of life' (1958:37); it flourishes only in what she describes as the sphere of freedom, and not the sphere of necessity, of everyday, practical life. Yet twentieth-century politics has become dominated by the lesser ideals that are born out of poverty and deprivation – the desire for abundance and the obsession with consumption and material need. In the process, 'the individual has got the better of the citizen' (1963:137), and politics has almost disappeared. Governments are now judged primarily in terms of how well they serve our material interests and how careful they have been to leave us in peace. The idea that politics is about the pursuit of *public* happiness or the taste for *public* freedom has been tossed aside as an archaic ideal. Instead of associating freedom with active participation, we have come to think of it as something threatened by the political realm; we treat government as a necessary evil, but an evil nonetheless.

Arendt is unashamedly captivated by the politics of the ancient world, though she knows full well that citizen involvement was premised on excluding women and slaves. 'The Greeks, whose city-state was the most individualistic and least conformable body politic known to us, were quite aware of the fact that the *polis*, with its emphasis on action and speech, could survive only if the number of citizens remained restricted' (1958: 43). And while she hardly proposes to return us to this, she does warn that the political passions and political qualities are not equally distributed among us all, and that those who volunteer themselves for public business (which is absolutely not the same as manoeuvring for a political career) can justifiably claim an authority in running public affairs. It does not, in other words, matter if a vast majority excludes itself from political activity and debate so long as this is *self*-exclusion. A political elite is entirely legitimate, and in the true sense of elite, what we need.

In this aspect of her thinking, Arendt is hardly representative, but her preoccupations are more widely shared where she criticizes the workplace ideal. It is, she suggests, one thing to call for decentralized units of local democracy – the kind of soviets or councils or communes that are briefly thrown up by every revolution, and then ruthlessly disbanded when they find themselves at odds with the party in control – but quite another to agitate for work-based councils as if this has anything to do with what democracy involves. The fatal mistake of those who advocate workers' councils, she argues, is not to 'distinguish clearly between participation in public affairs and administration or management of things in the public interest' (1963:277–8). Those who are good at the one are not necessarily good at the other. This may sound like the conventional point that when we elect managers we do not always get those who are 'best' at the job, but the issues Arendt raises are more thought-provoking than that. Along with later theorists like Sheldon Wolin or Benjamin Barber, she sees politics as the moment when we stand back from the pressures and materialism of everyday life, and think beyond our personal needs. In her sense of politics, a neighbourhood council might possibly lay claim to the term, because it deals with the shared and general concerns that affect all the community's groups, but certainly not a workplace committee, which deals by definition with specific and administrative affairs.

For many years this was also the position of Sheldon Wolin, who dismissed the contemporary interest in the community or the organization as a search for 'substitute love-objects for the political' (1960:368) and poured considerable scorn on what he saw as parochial, non-political concerns. He has since shifted to a slightly more accommodating position. Noting in 1982 the 'astonishing' range and variety of grass-roots movements that in all the areas of health care, education, environment and nuclear power were contesting authoritarian control, he stresses their vitality and democratic importance. But he goes on:

> While it is of the utmost importance that democrats support and encourage political activity at the grassroots level, it is equally necessary that the political limitations of such activity be recognized. It is politically incomplete. This is because the localism that is the strength of grassroots organizations is also their limitation. There are major problems in our society that are general in nature and necessitate modes of vision and action that are comprehensive rather than parochial. And there are historical legacies of wrong and unfairness that will never be confronted and may even be exacerbated by exclusive concern with backyard politics. (Wolin 1982:27–8)

For an advocate of republican democracy, the problem with liberalism is not just that it limits the space for political activity, or that it relies on passive acquiescence instead of substantial consent. Equally damning is the way it has legitimated a politics of self-interest. The state has become a bustling terminus for passengers intent on their own destination, the art of politics a matter of sorting out timetables and getting as many trains as possible to arrive on time. Common interest has been turned into common denominator, so that instead of raising our sights to general considerations it drags us down towards the most mundane. From this angle, the problem is how to repoliticize the public, how to get us out of our parochial, all too private concerns. The participatory model is useful enough when it stresses the crisis of passivity and the lack of participation, but it goes sadly awry when it pursues its solutions into the 'little' world of workshop or housing estate or school. The more local the participation, the more likely it is to reproduce interest group politics, and leave us still stuck in our own backyard.

Feminism and republicanism There is little in this that meets with contemporary feminist concerns, though one minor point of convergence is the distaste for a politics based on interest. A number of feminists have suggested that the notion of 'interest' reflects the poverty of the masculine world (Diamond and Hartsock 1981), and in doing so have picked up on themes long part of the feminist tradition. From the suffrage movement onwards, women have frequently seen themselves as bringing a greater generosity into politics, so that even in pressing for the interests of women, they would be subverting the assumption that politics is about looking after yourself. The recurrent equation women have made between their 'interests' and those of children is one example of this; the links some now see between feminism and the defence of the environment is another. This emphasis coexists with what is almost the reverse: the women's movement has also argued against the self-denying altruism that kept women silent over their own interests and needs, and in this sense has called on women to see that they have interests of their own. The critique of interest-led politics is then one strand among many, but where it holds, it builds a fragile bridge towards the preoccupations of republican democracy. In all other aspects, republicanism and feminism appear to be diametrically opposed.

Liberalism has at least struggled to accept women into the category of individuals, even if it remains impaled on the nature of the individual itself. Participatory democracy has at least allied with the contemporary women's movement in a common commitment to spreading democracy around and, despite its blinkered emphasis on the workplace, shares many recent feminist concerns. With the determined emphasis it places on universal as opposed to particular concerns, and the sharp separation it makes between public and private, republicanism looks the most impervious to gender. While contemporary feminists have been insisting on the differences between us, representatives of this last tradition have turned their attention the opposite way.

There is now a substantial literature, including Nancy Hartsock's *Money, Sex and Power* (1983), Mary O'Brien's *Politics of*

Reproduction (1981) and Genevieve Lloyd's *Man of Reason* (1984), which challenges the association between 'politics' and what is abstract, general or ideal; it suggests that the repeated dichotomies between reason and nature, abstract and concrete, freedom and necessity, public and private, account for much that is inadequate in orthodox theory. For Nancy Hartsock, for example, the hierarchical dualisms through which we think our political and theoretical life are grounded in the differential experience of boys and girls. The boy finds no model for himself in the family and has to get out to become a real man. 'Masculinity must be attained by means of opposition to the concrete world of daily life, by escaping from contact with the female world of the household into the masculine world of politics or public life.' This means that the public sphere is defined through its contrast with the private, and in this opposition, the one is 'valuable, if abstract and deeply unattainable, the other useless and demeaning' (Hartsock 1983: 241).

I am stuck by the curious dislocation, however, between feminist critiques of this 'transcendent public' and the very strong sense writers like Arendt or Wolin convey of struggling to stem a tide. Those writers who most clearly conform to the dualist opposition between the glories of politics and the ordinariness of everyday life have felt themselves to be arguing against the mood of their time; far from trusting to their position as a dominant (male) perspective, they have seen themselves defending what they fear is now lost. And on this point I believe they are right. In the current reassertions of the market over planning, governments increasingly appeal to the elusive sovereignty of the consumer as more democratic and enabling than processes of political decision-making, and the vision that underlies this shift in consensus could well be described as 'the depreciation of the politicalness of the political order' (Wolin 1960:431). With the 'fiscal crisis' or 'overloading' of the state in Western democracies, public utilities have been sold off to become private concerns; and even in such seemingly social matters as health, education, transport or housing, the cumbersome apparatus through which public bodies have attempted to sustain a semblance of principled provision has been dismissed as inefficient, irrelevant or unfair. Armed with a knowledge of the competing wares, individuals are increasingly called on to make their own decisions, and any schools or hospitals which fall by the wayside in the rush to choose the best on display will only be getting their (much delayed) just deserts. As this pattern potentially repeats itself throughout Eastern Europe, politics is being subordinated to society with a vengeance; democracy is being redefined in consumerist terms.

The critique of the welfare state in Western Europe potentially combines with the critique of the command economy in Eastern Europe to erode still further the sphere of public life. The 'political' is surely in a sorry condition, and a crucial part of the concern for democracy is the desire to see this reversed. Liberal democracies generally meet the minimum requirements, guaranteeing equal rights to vote, the freedom to form political parties and the formal (if not practical) right to put yourself forward as a candidate for office. What many people feel is that this gives them little or no power, either because decisions have been taken out of the political realm and into the anonymous, unaccountable corridors of major corporations, or because they have no influence or purchase on what politicians might choose to do. As Jürgen Habermas noted many years ago, the public realm is more and more 'confined to spectacles and acclamation' (1971:75), so that it becomes a matter of 'public relations' or something we just watch on TV. And listening to analysis of current affairs, it often seems that crucial decisions over domestic and foreign policy hinge on the most irrelevant of absurdities: the 'strength' or 'weakness' of political personalities; their agility in dealing with press and TV; their 'success' or 'failure' in major speeches; even, in America, their height. How can any of this preamble to elections be described as the exercise of popular choice?

These are troubling issues, and feminists cannot afford to stand aside from them. So is there any room for manoeuvre between the republican and feminist traditions? Iris Young is particularly interesting in this respect, for she combines a belief that 'emancipatory politics requires generating a renewed sense of public life' (1987:73) with an argument for heterogeneity and difference. Political thinkers, she notes, are always presenting us with an ideal of universal citizenship. The good thing about this is that it suggests everyone should be regarded as a citizen; the bad thing is that it gets conflated with a notion of homogeneity, where we must 'forget' what makes us different, and can only aspire to being treated the same. Far from leading to a genuinely common interest, this merely secures the dominance of privileged groups, for they then dress themselves in universal guise:

In a society where some groups are privileged while others are oppressed, insisting that as citizens persons should leave behind their particular affiliations and experiences to adopt a general point of view serves only to reinforce that privilege; for the perspectives and interests of the privileged will tend to dominate this unified public, marginalizing or silencing those of other groups. (Young 1989:257)

The idea that universality can conceal particular interests links up with the arguments against the abstractions of the liberal 'individual'. Iris Young is pursuing a similar point, but this time to challenge Benjamin Barber, as a modern-day republican male. Barber has built his case for *Strong Democracy* on a notion of transcendence, on people getting out of themselves and discarding their more private concerns. The minimal democracy of liberalism allows us only to register existing interests or needs, and treats our interests as pre-given, frozen affairs. Against this, Barber argues for a politics that is defined through activity and change. Politics exists precisely where there is no absolute guide, no ultimate truth. It is what we do 'when metaphysics fails' (1984: 131). It is the mechanism through which we transcend our various class or racial identities (he does not mention gender, but presumably the same points would apply). The narrow preoccupations with which we entered the citizens' assembly will be transformed, and in having to recognize wider considerations, we will come to see things in a more public light.

This is an excellent example of contemporary republican thinking, and for Iris Young it simply reinforces the pressures that try to make us conform. In an argument that has much in common with Carole Pateman or Zillah Eisenstein, she appeals instead to heterogeneity and difference and calls on us to revise our notions of justice so that they no longer impose a unitary norm. Justice should not, she argues, be conceived as impartial, as something that transcends our particular needs and concerns. 'Recent feminist analyses of the dichotomy between public and private in modern political theory imply that the ideal of the civic public as impartial and universal is itself suspect' (1987:66). Instead of putting abstract justice in one corner (usually male) and sympathy and feeling in another (usually female) we need to bring these together. Instead of dismissing from the public arena everything that makes us peculiar, specific or different, we should be exploring this heterogeneity in order to enhance our understanding of what it is we share. Iris Young argues, for example, for building into our political system some representation for oppressed groups, who would then have a right to be heard in contexts where policy affecting their group was being decided. More strongly and controversially, these groups should also have veto power over those policies that directly affect them. Two examples she suggests here are that women should have veto power over decisions relating to reproductive rights; and Native Americans veto power over the use of reservation lands (1989:262).

I shall explore aspects of this last suggestion in the next chapter, when I look at the representation of women as a group. For the moment let me note that Iris Young is not arguing against all aspects of the republican tradition, but (like Hannah Pitkin in her analysis of Machiavelli) is trying to rescue the best of the tradition from its current blindness to gender. Thus, she suggests, her proposals on the representation of oppressed groups could go some way towards meeting republican concerns for, once the principle of *group* representation is accepted, this could prove 'the best antidote to self-deceiving self-interest masked as impartial or general interest' (Young 1989:263). The bleak world of bargains and deals could then give way to a repoliticized public life. The point she stresses is that this can happen adequately enough through the fact that we engage in politics, that we have to recognize others and reach a decision that seems fair and just. We do not also need a 'general perspective', for this general perspective is an establishment myth.

Universality or difference? Liberalism, along with its offspring liberal democracy, has presumed that we can abstract some 'core' humanity from all the complexities and differences of real life, and it is to this essential person that liberals then offer their democratic rights. Universality is in this sense what grounds liberal theory; it is something with a prior existence that theory will enable us to capture as the basis for our principles and rights. For those influenced by civic republicanism, universality acts more as a vision for the future, the condition to which we aspire. And at its best, universal citizenship is what every oppressed group has appealed to over the last two hundred years: 'No it doesn't matter that I am a woman or an African or a Jew, for what matters is that we are all human beings.' At its worst, however, it suffers from what generations of socialists have pointed out in relation to class: it denies what are very real (social) differences that will prevent us from being treated the same. But at least the socialist criticism can be dealt with without abandoning everything 'the individual' or 'the citizen' implies. If recent feminist arguments are right, we have to jettison any kind of concept that abstracts from the body, for no one abstraction can serve for us all.

This is the point at which the contemporary malaise with grand theory unites in seeming harmony with the feminist emphasis on sexual difference. Through the 1970s and into the 1980s, political theory was dominated by radical abstractions. John Rawls's *A Theory of Justice* called on us to imagine ourselves stripped of all characteristics or qualities and, from behind this 'veil of ignorance', to work out what kind of distributive principles would be just. Robert Nozick's *Anarchy, State and Utopia* more summarily informed us that certain individual rights were inviolate and paramount, holding through all variations of place and time. This severity towards the muddle of everyday existence was in sharp contrast to the cosy commonplaces that had previously characterized much of political philosophy. But the tide has since turned again, towards a 'communitarian' emphasis on the social context that provides us with our moral and political values, and an anti-metaphysics that sees the 'self' as having no substance apart from the characteristics that Rawls stripped away. Rawls has since restated his theory in terms more acceptable to these critics, arguing that the project of his work was always political rather than metaphysical, and that his aim was 'to identify the kernel of an overlapping consensus, that is, the shared intuitive ideas which when worked up into a political conception of justice turn out to be sufficient to underwrite a just constitutional regime' (1985:246–7). He was elucidating ideas already present, not trying to deduce a grand theory from scratch.

As communitarianism achieves wider circulation, the question raised by a series of critics (for example, Gutmann 1985, Green 1985b) is whether it can offer enough critical edge on the societies in which we live. What is the difference between elucidating 'shared intuitive ideas' and simply repeating a dominant ideology? If we abandon the metaphysics of (say) universal rights, can we do more than reflect a consensus? What scope is there for criticizing inequality or subordination if the (unequal) community provides the standards from which we judge? Consider Michael Walzer, whose *Spheres of Justice* begins with a disclaimer of any metaphysical intent. 'My argument', he insists, 'is radically particularist. I don't claim to have achieved any great distance from the social world in which I live' (1983:xiv). What matters to him is drawing out the various shared understandings through which people live their lives. The reader is continually referred to a notion of what 'we' consider fair or just or appropriate, and Walzer explicitly defends this procedure as the only way to deal with the possible as opposed to ideal: 'Justice and equality can conceivably be worked out as philosophical artefacts, but a just or egalitarian society cannot be. If such a society isn't already here – hidden as it were, in our concepts and categories – we will never know it concretely or realize it in fact' (p. xiv). As Philip Green notes, the potential radicalism is that Walzer is concerned with 'latent structure' rather than 'overt manifestation' (1985b:989); but when 'most of "our shared understandings" . . . are not nearly as shared as Walzer sometimes seems to imply' (p. 992), does this radicalism go far enough? Green goes on to suggest that it is over issues of racial and sexual subordination that people can least put their trust in a latent consensus, and must rely most urgently on their abstract, universal rights.

Similar points have been raised in debate with Richard Rorty, who writes with a defiant parochialism of those beliefs on which 'we' are likely to agree. In *Contingency, Irony and Solidarity*, Rorty argues that liberalism can and now should abandon its universal pretensions. Instead of thinking that human solidarity rests on some absurdly metaphysical notion of what we all have in common, liberals should recognize that it is created by imaginative identification, and best served by the literary narratives that make it 'more difficult to marginalize people different from ourselves' (1989:xvi). So, like many contemporary feminists, Rorty has no time for the abstractions of humanity, the essential individual, the universal ideal. Like many conservative thinkers, he sees all our more general sympathies and obligations as building up from the locality from which we start. Not surprisingly, he has been accused of ethnocentrism, and his main defence is that he is describing what we do. For most of us it is indeed the direct contact of meeting and conversing with people, combined with the literary contact of reading about them, that helps extend our circle of sympathies to embrace those we once thought incomprehensible. The metaphysics of 'humanity as such' no longer works in the same old way.

One difficulty with this, as Richard Bernstein (1987) has noted, is that ethnocentrism can be pernicious as well as benign. Rorty comments, for example, that if American liberals want to secure support for policies that will help alleviate the hopelessness and misery of young blacks in American cities, then 'it is much more persuasive – morally as well as politically – to describe them as our fellow *Americans*' (Rorty 1989:191). Others may feel that the potential gains are not enough to justify the risks and that a politics that could legitimize nationalist exclusion is not going to be worth it in the end. The fact that people find it easier to identify with what is closest to them does not establish conclusively the irrelevance of any grander ideal. Nor does the fact that people might smuggle into what is meant to be universal a more limited reflection of themselves.

Think, for example, of the events surrounding the publication of Salman Rushdie's *The Satanic Verses*, a novel that provoked a storm of protest within Muslim communities for its supposedly blasphemous presentation of the prophet. Within months, Rushdie had been forced into hiding under a sentence of death proclaimed by the Ayatollah Khomeini; and in India a number of people died in demonstrations against the book. Though people spoke out powerfully in defence of publication, there was also a marked loss of confidence over what freedom of speech should mean. In the canon of liberal democracy, the right to freedom of expression has been regarded as one of the most basic principles, as has the right to pursue one's religion as one wishes, without interference from others or the state. The problem raised here was not that the two rights were now shown to be in conflict. The difficulty rather was that the underlying notion of fairness seemed to rely on applying the lowest common denominator. It has been a key principle of liberalism that all individuals and groups should be treated equally. There should be no preference in favour of any one religion, or indeed of religion at all: all opinions should be dealt with in an even-handed way, with no favouritism towards one over another. This is the theory, not the practice, for every country imposes some form of censorship; and, in the case of Britain, blasphemy is defined in exclusively Christian terms. But even assuming that such anomalies could be sorted out, is the theory what it ought to be?

One of the points made against the publication of *The Satanic Verses* was that the approach of the lowest common denominator favoured certain groups over others. Christianity has accommodated itself over the centuries to a tolerance that comes very close to agnosticism, but for better or worse other religions have retained their intensity of conviction. What is fair and just in one case might prove almost worse than nothing in the other, for while the idea that religion is something you get on with in your private life fits fine with one belief, it may be totally at odds with another; and while the injunction that irreverence and blasphemy should be ignored or simply shrugged off is in tune with the one, it is felt entirely out of place with the other. Liberal democracy tries to abstract from the content and practices of each religion and come up with a set of rules that can be applied equally to all. Yet, arguably, it has written the stance of *one* of these religions into its 'neutral' rules. Those who profess themselves unable to understand what the fuss is about ('you don't have to read the book if it bothers you so much') are perhaps refusing to engage with an experience that is different from their own. They are imposing a unitary norm.

This is an example that indicates both strengths and weaknesses of what some contemporary feminists argue. It confirms the point that impartiality is not just a matter of abstracting from difference in order to identify a lowest common denominator. The very idea that there *is* a lowest common denominator (in the case of citizenship, that it does not matter whether you are a woman or a man; in the case of religion, that it does not matter what you believe) turns out to be weighted in favour of certain groups. This is a problem. But one would not want to be propelled by this discovery into the opposite direction. In the case of the *Satanic Verses*, this could mean banning a novel because it offended certain groups, and giving legitimacy to the notion that its author should die. Democracy surely does imply tolerance of difference, and while agreeing with Iris Young that this cannot mean pretending away all differences that exist, it is nonetheless hard to conceptualize without some means of distancing ourselves from those qualities we used to think most intrinsic. Somehow or other, we have to be able to stand back from the things that are peculiar to us, whether it is our sex, our religion, our race or our political views, and try to think ourselves into another person's place. Part of the anxiety generated by fundamentalism – whether it is of a religious or political variety – is that it makes it impossible for its adherents to engage in this process, for even in principle they cannot treat their beliefs as detached.

The answer lies, I believe, in reversing the orthodox way of thinking about the relationship between 'accident' and 'core'. It is indeed a quaint metaphysics that distinguishes the essential – what Michael Sandel (1984) calls the 'unencumbered' – self from all the peculiarities and qualities and opinions that make us the people we are. It is, more pointedly, a political disaster, for as feminism has so clearly established, it writes into the abstractions of humanity the perspectives of the dominant group. But there is one aspect of this now beleaguered position that we cannot afford to lose, and that is the requirement for challenging and transforming the perspectives from which we have previously viewed the world. The mistake has been to see this process as one of delving behind the so-called accidents of being to come up with a purified core. The problem is better approached from the opposite direction: of being able, partly through comparison with those who are different, to reconceptualize what we had considered our core attributes as if they were accidents themselves. Being able, that is, to detach ourselves (however imperfectly and temporarily) from the crucial facts of our sex, our religion, our nationality, our beliefs, and enter imaginatively into an experience that is different from our own.

It is precisely because we are constituted by so many different characteristics – or as Rorty would put it, because we are a network of beliefs, desires and emotions that constantly reweaves itself (1983:586) – that this becomes possible. There is no 'core' self behind all our differences, but neither is there *one* difference that essentially constitutes our self. Thus, important as sexual/bodily identity is, it is not the only or defining characteristic of a person, for what will seem to be the most essential feature will change (and should change) with the issue at stake. This, in fact, is where I part company with the most radical theorists of sexual difference. The risks associated with an emphasis on difference arise when this is translated into *the* difference; and when the (entirely legitimate) argument for incorporating both male and female into political theory and practice translates into a notion that male and female are given and fixed. There is a curious way in which some recent feminist thinking falls foul of what it has so well and frequently criticized: having identified the false oppositions and dualities of previous theorists, it then ends up just reversing the terms. If men have dealt only in abstract justice, let women be concrete and specific; if men have talked only of 'the individual' let women talk of real women and men. The approach works well enough as polemical correction, but it is too much of a mirror image of what it sets out to chastise. Where universality has been conceptualized as something that suppresses all individual and group difference, this is what needs to be changed: but not into an unmitigated celebration of 'the' difference.

What seems a core attribute in one context becomes incidental in another, and it is the capacity for thinking about and acting on this that makes it possible for people to relate. To this extent, we do want to 'leave our selves behind' when we engage in democratic politics: not in the sense of denying everything that makes us the people we are, but in the sense of seeing ourselves as constituted by an often contradictory complex of experiences and qualities, and then of seeing the gap between ourselves and others as in many ways a product of chance. The aspiration to universality is one possible description of this and, though I may stand accused, like Humpty-Dumpty, of just making the words mean what I choose, this is the sense in which I continue to employ the term.

3

THE REPRESENTATION OF
WOMEN

In the countries that lay claim to the title of democracy, women
have enjoyed many decades of formal equality, sharing with men
the right to vote, to stand in elections, to compete for any office
(political – not yet religious) in the land. Their participation in
voting is now much the same as men's. Yet almost regardless of
the date at which women won their rights (ranging from 1902 in
Australia, 1919 in West Germany, 1920 in the USA, 1928 in the
UK, to the much delayed 1971 in Switzerland), there has been a
marked consistency in the figures for female participation in
national and local politics. With the major recent exception of the
Nordic countries (to which I shall return), women figure in national politics at something between 2 and 10 per cent; in Britain and
the USA, women have found it notoriously hard to break the 5 per
cent barrier.

Figures for local politics are only marginally more promising. By
1983, women representatives had captured 13 per cent of the seats
on West German local councils; 14 per cent on the French conseils
municipaux; 14.4 per cent on county councils in England and
Wales; 11.1 per cent on regional councils in Scotland; and 7.9 per
cent on district councils in Northern Ireland (Lovenduski 1986). By
1985, women made up 14 per cent of the membership of municipal
and township governing boards in the United States, but had
been elected to mayor in only four of the hundred largest cities
(Randall 1987:105). The percentages are nothing to write home
about, and women's relatively higher profile in local politics only
confirms what is frequently observed: that the numbers rise where

the power of the office is less. We all know there are more men than women in politics, but the details still come as a shock: only forty-three women out of 650 members of the British parliament? Only twenty-eight women out of 435 members of the US House of Representatives? What kind of democracy is this?

Liberal democracy makes its neat equations between democracy and representation, democracy and universal suffrage, but asks us to consider as irrelevant the composition of our elected assemblies. The resulting pattern has been firmly skewed in the direction of white middle-class men, with the under-representation of women only the starkest (because they are half the population) among a range of excluded groups. The campaign for women's right to vote was always linked to a parallel campaign for women's right to be elected. Success in the first has not brought much joy in the second.

In even bothering to discuss this problem, I go against the grain of much contemporary feminism, and not only because of the theoretical challenges that have been levelled at liberal democracy. When the women's movement re-emerged in the late 1960s, there was a strong presumption in favour of direct democracy. This combined with a critical repudiation of party politics (returning the compliment to those parties who so long and happily ignored the women) to encourage scepticism towards orthodox channels. 'Getting women into politics', where politics meant parliament or national assembly, was very low down the list, and the real issues of democracy and participation were thought to lie elsewhere. Not that anyone would object if women were suddenly elected *en masse* to councils and parliaments: the celebrations would be boisterous enough for an achievement beyond most feminist dreams. But this then is part of the point. Until recently, no feminist in her right mind would have thought liberal democracy could deliver the goods, and since this coincided with a preference for more direct forms of participation, many just left it at that. The respectable agitations of bodies like the British 300 Group seemed to rest on a double naivety: the belief that substantially more women *could* get into Parliament without a prior revolution in social and sexual relations; and the equally odd notion that 300 women MPs would make a significant difference. In more academic circles, the literature on 'women in politics' (more accurately, women not in politics) operated perilously close to the threshold of boredom. For those who knew that women were oppressed, the dreary statistics lacked any element of surprise. The common-sense explanations for women's low profile held little appeal for minds still buzzing with the latest theoretical fashions.

The under-representation of women within conventional politics is nonetheless crucial in thinking about democracy and gender. The general critique of liberal democracy leaves a teasing vacuum on what could serve as alternatives, while the questions raised over the two most common alternatives suggest that neither can be simply adopted in its place. We can perhaps move on to more substantial ground if we examine more closely the weaknesses (and possibly strengths) of current liberal democratic practice. What does the under-representation of women add to the understanding of democracy? It shows that there is a problem undoubtedly, but is the problem then in the theory or application? Setting aside for the moment what may be more fundamental problems with liberal/representative democracy, can we anticipate a trend towards sexual parity? Is there a theoretical problem with the 'representation of women', an incongruity between this and the assumptions of liberal democracy? And following on the questions posed in chapter 1, does feminism provide us with a novel angle on these issues, a different way of conceiving either possibilities or limits? There are two major aspects of this, which I shall discuss in separate sections. What are the theoretical issues implied in the notion of representation? What are the chances of electing more women?

'Mirror' representation Confront people with the damning evidence on the number of women elected and they tend to divide into those who think this matters and those who say it does not. Much of the disagreement reflects the complacency, not to say dishonesty, of those who enjoy a monopoly of power, but there are more intriguing issues at stake. As with many feminist demands, the case for greater parity in politics has been made in three ways (Hernes 1987). Part of it relies on a notion of basic justice, and fits within a broad sweep of arguments that challenges sexual segregation wherever it occurs. Just as it is unjust that women should be cooks but not engineers, typists but not directors, so it is unjust that they should be excluded from the central activities in the political realm; indeed, given the overarching significance of politics, it is even more unfair that women should be kept out of this. But for the hundred years and more that access to political power has been an issue, women's organizations have combined the case for justice with at least one additional point. Sometimes the argument is that women would bring to politics a different set of values, experiences and expertise: that women would enrich our political life, usually in the direction of a more caring, compassionate society. A more radical version is that men and women are in conflict and that it is nonsense to see women as represented by men.

The case for justice says nothing about what women will do if they get into politics, while the two further arguments imply that the content of politics will change. All unite in seeing a sexual disproportion between electors and elected as evidence that something is wrong. The striking homogeneity of our existing representatives is proof enough of this, since if there were no substantial differences between men and women, or between black people and white, then those elected would undoubtedly be a more random sample from those who elect. Consistent underrepresentation of any social category already establishes that there is a problem. Such a marked variance from the population as a whole could never be an accidental result. Leaving aside as mere prejudice the notion that women are 'naturally' indifferent to politics, there must be something that prevents their involvement. The argument from justice then calls on us to eliminate or moderate whatever obstacles we find to women's participation, while the arguments from women's different values or different interests go one stage further. The sexual differentiation in conditions and experience has produced a specifically woman's point of view, which is either complementary or antagonistic to the man's. Any system of representation which consistently excludes the voices of women is not just unfair; it does not begin to count as representation.

All three arguments are at odds with what has become the orthodoxy, for while there are a number of competing versions on offer, the idea that representatives should in some way 'mirror' those they represent is probably the most contested. The near universal practice of electing representatives according to geographical constituencies suggests that those elected are meant to speak for an area or a place, the implication being that interests are relatively homogeneous within localities, but potentially at odds between them. Whether the representatives are male or female would then be deemed irrelevant, though where there are concentrations of rich or poor, or areas populated by particular racial or religious groups, the class, race or religion of the representative might well be seen as important. Party selectorates do, as we know, like to choose candidates who seem consonant with the locality but, with exceptions such as Northern Ireland where there is a clear conflict by religion, and perhaps inner city constituencies where the voters are more homogeneous in their class or their race, this version of representation is largely thought an anachronism.

The classic challenge to it derives from Edmund Burke's speech to the electors of Bristol, where he argued that representatives should serve not local interests but the nation, and should therefore be free to exercise their own judgement on political affairs. Here, too, sex is out of the picture, or perhaps, more precisely, enters to the disadvantage of women. The Burkean representative is a man of honour, integrity and breadth of vision. The process that produced him is merely the gesture meritocracy makes to democratic beliefs; what matters is that he should be 'better' than the voters who put him there.

The subsequent growth of the party system has legitimated yet another view: that those elected are to speak for their supporters' opinions or beliefs. The most radical versions of this will argue for strong mechanisms of accountability or recall, noting that if MPs and councillors are supposed to represent our political views, they should be bound or mandated to the policies we support. But except when issues of gender have entered into party programmes, there is no explicit presumption among either radicals or moderates in favour of either sex. The fact that most of those elected turn out to be men might be noted or deplored, but it is the ideas not the people that count.

The dominant practice in most contemporary democracies is a muddled combination of both accountability and autonomy. Our representatives are said to represent our views (political parties present us with alternative policies, and we make a choice between them), but only in the vaguest of ways (election manifestos offer bland generalities, and those elected then fill in the details themselves). Those elected are seen as carrying some responsibility for their area, but are not permitted to take this too far, for they are ultimately bound by party lines. On any of the major social or demographic characteristics (age, sex, race, class) they do not represent us at all. Taking the example of British Members of Parliament: lawyers make up the largest single occupational group; women have only just pushed beyond five per cent of the total; and the proportion of the population that is non-white is currently 'represented' by a mere handful of MPs, whose election in 1987 marked the first substantial breach in the white monopoly.

Those who challenge the system which produces this are usually faced with a form of *reductio ad absurdum* that queries how far the principle of proportionality should go. Are we supposed to elect students, pensioners, the unemployed, in numbers that mirror their proportion in society? Are we supposed to have proportional representation of every occupational classification, every religion, every racial and linguistic minority? Are we supposed to do five-yearly investigations into the number of lesbians and homosexuals in order to ensure their fair representation in parliament? And what about height, weight, hair colour, tastes in music or sport or books? The whole idea is patently absurd.

Representative democracy cannot produce a perfect reflection of society: the only guarantee of that would be all the citizens meeting together in national assembly. Within the limits of representation, it is hard to see how to get agreement on the categories to be covered. Even where such agreement becomes possible, proportionality inevitably reduces local autonomy, for it must involve some form of national party directive over the kind of candidates each constituency should choose. But arguments that rely on the impossibility of one extreme in order to justify its opposite are always suspect, and as long as those who speak for us are drawn from such an *un*representative sample, then democracy will remain profoundly flawed. The obstacles that deny certain people the chance of election are as undemocratic in their way as the laws that once excluded them from the right to vote. And moving on to the more positive point, different experiences do create different values, priorities, interests; while we may all be capable of that imaginative leap that takes us beyond our own situation, history indicates that we do this very partially, if at all. Those who regard the current situation with complacency are not too far in spirit from the nineteenth-century apologists of male suffrage, who claimed that a man spoke for himself and 'his' woman, and thus that the woman had no need for a separate voice. Where there are different interests and different experiences, it is either naive or dishonest to say that one group can speak for us all.

What we see as the salient differences will of course vary through history. In contemporary Britain, for example, it may not seem of much moment whether the proportions of Catholics, Protestants or Jews elected fairly reflect the proportions in society as a whole. It has certainly mattered in the past, and in the case of Muslims it is beginning to matter a great deal. The prevailing terms of contemporary politics suggest the triad of sex, race and class as the dominant fissures, but I do not insist on these as exclusive. Political movements establish which categories are important; comparisons of those elected with a random sample of those who elect alert us to what is usually a yawning divide. It does not detract from the seriousness of the case to note that this will throw up the odd aberration. Until it was pointed out to me that those elected to the presidency of the United States are not just white and male but tall, it had not occurred to me that height could be a salient consideration. I now take this as confirming the equation between politics and men, which casts its shadow over those who fall short of the masculine ideal.

Group representation The extraordinary under-representation of women must be considered a problem. But how close does this bring us to agreeing a solution? The strongest conclusion – particularly where the argument is based on the conflicting interests of women and men – is that there should be women representing the interests of women, workers representing the interests of workers, black people representing the interests of black people, and so on. This is indeed argued in other areas (reserved seats for women, for example, on party or trade union executives) but no one to my knowledge puts the case for this in national affairs. We may talk of the representation of workers by working-class MPs, or black people by black MPs, but in most cases this is conceptual slippage, for there are some constituencies that are overwhelmingly working class, and others with a very substantial black population. In such conditions it is possible to see working-class or black MPs as 'representing' their class or race, even when in principle they are supposed to represent their party or more generally the people in their constituency. (The combination proves easier with class than with race: in British politics there are working-class MPs from working-class constituencies who will proclaim unequivocally that they are there to represent their class; while the recently elected black MPs have been at pains to insist that they do not 'just' speak for black people, but for all the voters – black and white – in their constituency.)

With women this kind of slippage is ruled out from the start. There are no geographical concentrations that could form the basis for a 'women's constituency', and as long as voting is tied to localities, no woman candidate can seriously present herself as representing women alone. At an informal level it may be felt appropriate that our national assemblies should contain some farmers, some housewives, some manual workers. But once suggest that these individuals are there to 'represent' only these groups, and the howls of outrage will send you scurrying for cover.

Setting aside the entirely dishonest example of apartheid in South Africa, the only precedents that formally institutionalize 'organic' representation relate to minority ethnic groups. The four Maori seats in the New Zealand House of Representatives are a striking case in point (McLeay 1980). Introduced as a short-term measure in 1867 because so few Maoris qualified to vote under the property-based male franchise, the system of separate representation has survived intact to the present day. The four constituencies are geographically defined, though each covers a much larger area than the 'European' ones; and since 1975 it has been open to all people of Maori descent to choose whether to register on the Maori or General roll. The system of reserved seats is now defended as a means of preserving Maori culture and representing the most disadvantaged group in society, and as the recent Commission on Electoral Reform (1986) suggests, it is the cultural differentiation that underpins the case. If the interests of Maoris related exclusively to poor housing, inadequate health provision, high unemployment, under-resourced schools, they would be on a continuum with the needs and desires of all New Zealanders, and more readily abandoned to the usual battles between parties. But once the preservation of Maori culture and identity is admitted as a legitimate goal, then the notion that there must be Maoris to speak for the Maori point of view becomes more widely accepted.

The 1986 commission did accept this, but not the implication that Maoris should have reserved seats. The system has guaranteed a minimum of four Maori MPs in a legislature that currently has 95 seats – not an impressive fraction when those of Maori descent make up 9 per cent of the population, though quite likely better than would otherwise be achieved. Has it done anything more? Since 1943 the Labour Party has consistently won all four of the seats, and the argument is that this *de facto* monopoly reduces the incentive for anyone to promote Maori concerns. Outside the Labour Party there are minimal rewards for pursuing Maori interests; inside the party the rewards are secure without any further effort. Cynics would predict that of the two major political parties in New Zealand, the National Party will favour abolishing the separate seats and the Labour Party will support their retention. Cynics would be absolutely right. The only aberration is that the National Party has bothered to select Maori candidates for two winnable seats in the European constituencies, but this, too, is open to comment. If the party is to make its case for abolishing what is variously described as a special privilege and an insult to the Maoris, it has to show that Maoris can still be elected MPs.

Arguing for Maori representation but against the existing safe seats, the Royal Commission 'assumes that the representation of groups in Parliament – whether it is talking about political parties, special interests or minority groups – ought to mirror the distribution of opinion and group identity in the general community' (McLeay 1987:87). It is the emphasis on group identity that is the interesting one. Everyone would say that our representatives ought to reflect the distribution of opinion: when parties fight elections that is what elections are supposed to be about. Should they also reflect 'group identity'?

Norberto Bobbio has argued that 'organic' or 'sectional' representation is entirely appropriate and desirable in more localized contexts: workers' interests should be represented by workers on factory committees; students' interests should be represented by students on college faculty committees. 'But once the context changes to where what is at stake are the interests of the citizen and not those of this or that interest group, citizens should be represented by citizens who are distinguished from each other on the grounds, not of the interest groups they represent, but of the different general visions they have developed which inform the way they conceive the problems' (1984:51). What would he say about the representation of Maoris? Or that rather more substantial 'minority' of women? His argument could perhaps accommodate a Women's Party, which presented to the electorate a general vision founded in the perception of women's interests and needs, but seems antagonistic to the idea of women being represented *as women* – and is a million miles away from any notion of women voting in women's elections for women MPs.

The problems of sectional representation are much debated in contemporary writing on democracy and, with all the wide variation, there seems to be general agreement that it is damaging at national level. Unlikely bedfellows in other respects, Edmund Burke and Norberto Bobbio are united over this point, Burke stressing the dangerous parochialism of the locality, Bobbio the blinkered egoism of interest-defined groups. It is the grain of truth in Burke's position (which otherwise, as Anthony Arblaster notes in his *Democracy* (1987:84), is not about representation at all) that local interests and local constituencies are limited in vision, and that if each representative speaks only for the locality, we are refusing responsibility for more general concerns. No one wants the motorway through her back garden; no one wants the travellers' camp at the end of his street. If we were able to talk through our interests and prejudices, we might be able to achieve an amicable solution, but representative democracy does not assist us in that. What happens is that our representatives talk to one another, and in the process come to believe that we who elected them were wrong. I am putting a generous gloss on this, for they probably assumed our foolishness from the start, but this is only to highlight the point. Representation by local geography can be the most conservative option of all, for while there may not be a 'nation' in the Burkean sense, there are certainly non-local interests that cry out to be met.

Representation by interest groups is not much better. In Norberto Bobbio's disenchanted view of the Italian parliamentary process, there is already too much lobbying by sectional interest, too little scope for general interests to emerge (see, for instance, Bobbio 1984:ch.2). The prospect of compounding this evil by giving it formal expression is anathema to him: ideas, not interests, are what politics should be about. Like others we have come across, he would like to see a democracy that transcends the grubby concerns of sectional groups: people as citizens, not as bearers of interest; politics as a matter of general concerns.

Given that women make up half the population, such reservations could be said to be beside the point. The critique of interest-led politics is a critique of minorities who lobby for themselves regardless of others and blind themselves to more generous concerns. Women are if anything a majority, and their interests are hardly a localized affair. At a practical level, however, the choice between supporting a woman because she is a woman and supporting a man who seems closer to your views constantly presents itself, and the theoretical issue that underlies this choice is one of the points at stake in thinking about 'representation'. I am not thinking here of the more extreme versions of this dilemma, for it is methodological individualism run wild to think that Margaret Thatcher as Prime Minister is better for women than some man who wants more nurseries or a higher minimum wage. But even within a single party the choice can arise – and even when the woman says she is speaking for women. Do we want the interests of women represented by women, or their needs and concerns by the party we support?

In the interests of women   One of the debates in contemporary feminist theory is whether women can be described as in interest-based group, whose interests then need representing. The argument began with Virginia Sapiro's 'When are interests interesting?' (1981), which set out to establish that the key issue is no longer women's right to be represented as individual women (their right to vote and stand in elections) but their representation as a group. Because of their materially different position in society, women have objectively different interests from men, but the entry of women as individual actors on the political scene does not mean that these interests are actively pursued. Though research suggests that women politicians develop different styles of political engagement, it also suggests that they are wary of speaking for women. So when policies that favour women have been introduced, it is as often as not a byproduct of changed circumstances (new labour market needs, for example) or of the fortunes of other social groups (equal opportunity policies were introduced in the United States with a view to tackling racial disadvantage, but they then applied to women as well). Getting more women elected may be a necessary but is certainly not a sufficient condition.

Later research offers more encouraging results on the stance of women politicians (see for instance, Hedlund 1988) and raises interesting questions about the numbers threshold at which women acquire the confidence to speak for their sex. But the debate has moved in a different direction, falling into what I have noted as the division between those who seek to incorporate an understanding of women into existing frameworks and those who see women as more fundamentally subversive. Thus Irene Diamond and Nancy Hartsock argue that the very language of rights and interests is grounded in the individualism of market society, an individualism of rational economic *men*. Feminist theory offers a 'clean break with the assumptions of the interest group framework' (1981:720), which they describe as centring on instrumental advantage and individual gain. The experience and concerns of women are said to transcend this, primarily because women's involvement in reproduction leads them to define them-

selves in more relational terms. It is not then a matter of representing the specific 'interests' of women (whether this means more
women in politics, or parties devoted to women's concerns); the
needs of women explode the whole politics of interest.

This is a risky case to argue, as is everything that relies on
women's special qualities or their different relationship to the
world. An emphasis on needs as opposed to interests can too
readily facilitate the belief that participation does not much matter
(Jonasdottir 1988); or that getting into politics is a male-defined
game and best left up to the boys. I am not saying that Diamond
and Hartsock reach this conclusion, but writing in the context of
the USA they are understandably disillusioned by the politics of
women's lobbying, which in a system that has given little formal
power to women as representatives, and few enough concessions
in material terms, has been the main public face of women's
'interests'. Others who adopt the notion of a specifically 'women's
culture' have fallen more definitely into the trap and explicitly
advise women against sharing male power.

When William Lafferty, for example, looks at the relatively low
participation of women in electoral politics, he explains it in terms
of a 'female culture' (1980, 1981). He considers the evidence that
women are actively kept out of politics as insufficient and relies
instead on the argument that they have a different value system.
Whereas men are predisposed to instrumental, interest-group
politics, women are drawn towards a more radical, non-
hierarchical politics, thus preferring to engage in direct action or
organize in specifically women's groups. (The basis of this difference is sometimes rather mysterious, with sex being presented as
an independent variable; at other times the difference is explained
by reference to women's reproductive role.) Since Lafferty
applauds women's alternative value system, he is reluctant to
promote changes that might weaken its effect. He argues that 'it
would be tragic indeed' if 'cooptation into the male game of
bargaining, manipulative power politics took place *before* women's
values were fully developed into the alternative cultural form they
give promise of . . . Ultimately, women will take their proportio-
nally equal place in the responsible constitutional governance of
the polity, but, in my opinion, there is definitely no hurry in this
area' (1981:162).

I find it hard to sympathize with this approach. Even in the
early days of the women's liberation movement, when getting
more women elected seemed such a secondary concern, I would

have baulked at the notion of there being 'no hurry' about any aspect of sexual equality. And while I would not go to the opposite extreme of claiming equal political participation as the one single issue that matters, I certainly think women need to be there. As Anna Jonasdottir has argued, there is at least one 'objective' interest we can confidently identify and that is women's interest in having a political presence: 'In no developed country have women reached the stage where they can give up the struggle for a real and controllable attendance as an identifiable group within the various groupings of society' (1988:57). The content of women's politics may well centre around need, and may turn out to express a different set of values that transcends the narrow egoism of interest. But unless women are actively present, and in numbers that will make them effective, they cannot even begin to act. Their needs might then be defined from above and not explored by the women themselves.

Women should be equally present in any elected assemblies with men, but the case for this may be weakened when linked to a notion that women represent women or express a specifically women's point of view. 'Women' has a deceptive simplicity which it takes from its opposition to 'men'. It implies a shared experience, crossing nation and race and class, and in the influential work of Robin Morgan (1984) it asserts that *Sisterhood is Global*. But this supposedly universal womanhood has provoked one of the major debates within feminism today. Bracketed within its general category are a multiplicity of real living women, who do not share an identical oppression; they have resisted the blandishments of what is supposed to be their movement to define themselves by their race, their class, their nationality, their age – anything and everything but their sex. After a brief and unhappy flirtation with the notion of false consciousness, feminists have taken this seriously, and many now argue that the division between women and men operates within and through what can be equally profound divisions among women. Chandra Talpade Mohanty, for example, argues that 'universal sisterhood, defined as the transcendence of the "male" world . . . ends up being a middle-class psychologized notion which effectively erases material and ideological power differences within and among groups of women, especially between first- and third-world women' (1987:38). Sexual inequality might be a universal phenomenon, but that does not mean women are universally the same.

Does it then make sense to talk of an objective common interest, or to speak of 'the' feminist demands? The least controversial route follows general formulations: Jonasdottir's 'formal' interest in participation; or Hege Skjeie's notion of access (Skjeie 1988). Since segregation is a fundamental ordering principle of gendered societies, women can be said to share at least one interest in common. They need improved access to every sphere. Beyond this we cannot too readily assume shared interests between women. We cannot say that women share a common 'interest' on such substantive issues as disarmament or ecology, or at any rate we cannot say they agree. We cannot even claim a clearly 'women's' perspective on such issues as abortion, for while surveys regularly report a difference in male and female attitudes, this is often that men are more liberal – or to put it another way, more cavalier. The experience of being a woman increases both the importance women attach to legalizing abortion *and* the reluctance they feel towards abortion itself. Each of these is a 'women's' perspective. Which of them should our representatives represent?

Accountability or trust? This brings me to a further problem that has been very little discussed. Within the framework of liberal democracy, elections are conducted on the basis of party competition, and while we may bemoan the poverty of electoral debate, we are supposed to be voting not for people but ideas. In the continuing battle between accountability and autonomy, the more democratic have usually sided with the principle of rendering accounts, arguing that this is what representation should mean. If the vote is to have any substance it must entail more than a preference for an individual we can trust: it should be a preference for a programme we support. We do not expect our representatives to turn round and tell us they've just had a brilliant idea but forgot to mention it when they asked for our votes. Or more cynically, we may well expect it, but we regard such behaviour as undemocratic and would never promote it as an ideal. Candidates are supposed to tell us their plans before the election and give us a chance to make up our minds. The fact that we vote for parties rather than individuals reflects this: instead of choosing between individuals on the basis of trust we choose between parties on the basis of their policies and ideals. Strong democrats mostly want to enhance rather than reduce this feature, and there is a long tradition that seeks to make representatives more accountable, to let the electorate decide on as much as is feasible and set the boundaries within which representatives can move.

The arguments over the representation of women have tended to evade this issue. Much recent literature has explored whether women representatives do indeed act differently from men, whether they adopt a different style of political behaviour, identify a different range of priorities, are more liberal or radical than men (for a recent overview, see Randall 1987:151–6). The implication is that we want them to be different, and that if they are not it undermines the case. As Vicky Randall puts it, 'it may be argued that we need to know more about the behaviour of women politicians, before deciding whether, as feminists, we want to increase their numbers' (p. 151). Yet within the general debates on democracy, this is an odd approach, for it suggests that once we have this evidence we will be happy to give our representatives a pretty free hand.

When a woman has been chosen as a candidate by her party and elected to carry through what her party represents, do we really want her to take it upon herself to say she 'speaks' for women, that she has a privileged understanding of women's special needs? Should she be setting herself up in opposition to her party, claiming a mandate derived from her sex? Is there not a tension between this and the accountability that democrats so widely espouse? As party activists and candidates, women can of course speak for women: they can agitate for party programmes or manifestos to include policies that reflect women's needs; they can make themselves experts in aspects of family or employment policy; they can serve as spokeswomen for feminist ideals. And on that vast range of topics that no party ever bothers to put before an electorate, women representatives can make themselves as free as the men to pursue the policies they favour. But we cannot have it both ways. We cannot challenge the Burkean notion of (non)-representation which sets the elected above the electors and lets them get on with what they know best; and at the same time treat women as if they have a special mission beyond party lines.

As long as the number of women elected is so pitiful, and the range of issues regarded as 'political' so male-defined, the dilemma will rarely emerge. Thus abortion has been considered a non-party issue in Britain, and feminists have been profoundly thankful for the handful of women MPs who have assumed a particular responsibility in debates on the topic. No one would accuse them of exceeding their representative role, or say that they were not elected to defend women's right to choose. In most cases the needs or interests of women have been so steadily overlooked by political parties that feminists are more anxious to hear women speak to these interests than to worry over their self-appointed role. What now seems an academic dilemma may, however, become important in the future. From the most minimalist to the most active, all theories of democracy deal with the question of popular control, and while the competition between political parties offers only limited mechanisms through which the electorate asserts its views (in the dourest versions, only the chance to say which party should govern), it does at least engage with the issue. In what sense, other than being women, can women say they represent women's views? Their legitimacy derives from election not nature, and any mandate in relation to women depends on the extent to which their parties – whether 'feminized' versions of existing parties or newly created women's parties – have argued explicitly for policies for women. Outside this mechanism, is it legitimate to say they represent their sex?

Think, for example, about what is implied in the following comments from Ingunn Norderval:

> Attempts to improve women's representation in legislative and party office ultimately confront the question, 'So what? Does women's presence in politics really matter?' Scandinavian arguments for increased numbers of females generally rely on three principles: First, democratic justice; second, resource utilisation; and third, interest representation. According to the first point, since women constitute roughly half the population, they are entitled to comparable numerical representation in those bodies which determine the laws under which they must live. The second position suggests that valuable human resources are wasted when women are not involved in politics; in this view, no society can afford to leave untapped half of its available talent.
>
> According to the third principle, which is increasingly popular in Scandinavia and elsewhere, women and men have different political interests because of gender-based differentiations throughout the social structure. Female exclusion from or under-representation in political activities therefore means that women's interests are poorly represented. Implicit in this third position is the assumption that women in politics do, or would, pursue different issues from men. (Norderval 1985:84)

I have no quarrel with the first point, or with the appeal to utilitarian sentiment, to say that more women would be a good thing. My difficulty lies with the third principle, for even if women do act differently from men, it is attributing tremendous powers to nature (or gender differentiation in the social structure) to assume that they will do what I would do in their place. Edmund Burke enjoined us to put our trust in those we elected, for they would know best what to do. The substitution of a woman for a man may allay some of the fears, but it still relies on trust rather than accountability or control.

Some degree of trust is, of course, inevitable, for the most rigid application of accountability would turn representatives into mere ciphers and would too seriously limit their responsibilities and role. I noted earlier that the current consensus in liberal democracies involves a muddled combination of accountability and autonomy: perhaps some degree of muddle is to be desired. People often comment on the poverty of parliamentary debate, where speeches resound in an empty chamber, or else are punctuated by a menagerie of noise as the cohorts of each party express their approval or disgust in a parody of serious debate. The extremes of accountability might make this worse, for if decisions were all dictated in the moment of election, the representatives would become mere numbers and not be expected to do anything more. If we want our representatives to act for us, we have to allow them some autonomy – and in the space this opens up, it will matter whether they are women or men. We should not, however, overstate this argument, for the issue of democracy keeps returning us to the problems of control.

Iris Marion Young's argument for the specific representation of oppressed groups is one of the few examples in contemporary feminist writing that does set out mechanisms for representation, though she is not concerned with numbers *per se*. Instead of focusing on the degree to which a legislature 'reflects' the sexual (or other) composition of a society, she argues that oppressed groups should have a guaranteed role in policy formation. The privileged can already rely on privileged access to the decision-making process. In the interests of democracy, we need procedures that will balance this out:

> Such group representation implies institutional mechanisms and public resources supporting three activities: (1) self-organization of group members so that they gain a sense of collective empowerment and a reflective understanding of their collective experience and interests in the context of the society; (2) voicing a group's analysis of how social policy proposals affect them, and generating policy

proposals themselves, in institutionalized contexts where decision-makers are obliged to show that they have taken these perspectives into consideration; (3) having veto power regarding specific policies that affect a group directly, for example, reproductive rights for women, or use of reservation lands for Native Americans. (1989: 261–2)

As the first condition rightly indicates, the notion of group representation must involve some context in which the group meets as a group – but then we are into the standard objection that meetings are unrepresentative and may only attract a minority of those entitled to attend. This is not a substantial problem as far as the second condition is concerned. The policy proposals may be generated by a minority, and it may not be clear whether other members of the group would agree. It still seems legitimate to demand that policy-makers should give these proposals their full consideration, and so far I support the suggestion. The difficulty lies with the final point. Should this group have a veto power?

Once the power over decisions is in question, then the precise mechanisms of accountability and the exact degrees of representation begin to matter. We want assurances that people speak for their group. If the veto is exercised through a series of meetings in which the group formulates its position, then exactly how representative will those meetings be? If the veto is exercised through a ballot of all members of the group, then what is to guarantee that they are voting in relation to their experience or interests as that group? None of the groups we might think of is homogeneous, and each will contain within itself a wide variety of competing views. We cannot therefore avoid questions of accountability and democratic control.

It is easy enough to show that women are under-represented in politics, and not too much more difficult to make the case that women are oppressed. On both counts something should surely be done. The disproportion between those elected and those who elect is too astounding to be attributed to accident, while the fact that it serves those who are already advantaged is too striking for any democrat to ignore. The difficulties arise in the next stage, for within the framework of representative democracy, it is political parties that have provided the vehicle for representation, and in its more substantial sense, the representation of women does not fit. 'Women' are not homogeneous and do not speak with a single voice.

Those who most vehemently opposed women's right to vote often feared that women would vote in a block and differently from men: that women's suffrage would disrupt the basis of party alignments by producing a new 'women's vote'; or, equally damning, that the new electors would prove more conservative than men and shift the previous balance between parties. This is, of course, why the leadership of the British Liberal Party was so resistant to votes for women, despite growing support within the Liberal rank and file; and why, in contrast, the leadership of the Conservative Party proved more sympathetic, despite horror and outrage in the party as a whole. As Millicent Fawcett put it, 'from the suffrage point of view, the [Liberal Party] was an army without generals, and the [Tory Party] was generals without an army' (quoted in Rosen 1974:12). As events turned out, a relatively minor 'gender gap' emerged, with women at first more inclined to vote for conservative parties, and more recently the other way round (see Mueller 1988). Those who resist an increase in women's representation no doubt harbour similar fears, anticipating that the women elected will alter the game. I hope there will be changes, but in the interests of democratic accountability these have to take place in the open, through the decision-making processes of each party and the publicity of electoral campaigns. We cannot jump too easily into the notion that there is an interest of women; and short of women's constituencies or women's elections, there is no clear mechanism for their representation.

The relative autonomy of politics Let me now turn the argument the other way. I have said that the case for more women representatives rests partly on a notion of equality in participation and partly on a notion of reflection, and that neither in principle nor in practice can this guarantee that women are then represented *as women*. We can anticipate that more women elected will shift the context and priorities of public policy, but cannot say this is necessarily so, nor indeed presume that their choices would win general acclaim. The problem may be even more acute. If feminists are right in the critiques they have developed of liberal democracy, then the nature of the public/private divide may make even equal numbers an impossible dream. If the constraints on women's political activity are set by their economic and social position, then the idea that you could have a parliament made up equally of men and women, without *also* having substantial changes in social relations, is nonsensical. The absurdity lies not in thinking that women would prove no different from men, but in imagining that they could ever get into such positions of power until after the changes were made. A democracy may require the policies on equality before the equality of representation – and yet without the second what hope is there of the first?

The question relates to parallel points that have been raised over class representation. Capitalist democracy offers the illusion of popular control: it suggests that we can elect representatives to promote our interests, and thereby change what has made us unequal. But the very inequalities militate against this, giving political power to those who already enjoy other powers. In their comparative study of *Participation and Political Equality* (1978) Verba, Nie and Kim document in intricate detail what everyone knows to be the case: that the extent to which individuals become involved in politics and thereby gain access to decision-making channels is directly correlated with the resources they have at their command; that all else being equal, those who have everything else get political power as well. The composition of our elected assemblies is only one aspect of this, but in terms of both class and gender it is a particularly marked one. Is the position of women in politics merely a subset of the general observation, or does it raise different issues?

Ten years ago I might have argued that the under-representation of women was an even more intractable problem than the under-representation of activists from the working class. In Britain there is at least one route, via trade union sponsorship of Labour Party candidates, for including working-class men. But with the recurrent failure to break through the numbers barrier there seemed little short of a revolution in domestic and work relations that would dent the male monopoly. Despite the higher profile of mainstream feminism in the USA, the American Congress has proved even worse. I am now more sanguine, not about the situation in Britain or the USA, which is dire, but about the extent to which specifically *political* change can secure greater equality of representation.

Explanations for women's relative invisibility in politics tend to be multi-causal – which is probably why I used to find them tedious, for they lack the drama of the singular cause. Women have been socialized into regarding politics as an alien affair; women are constrained by their responsibilities as mothers, and indeed their general role as carers for the young, sick and old, all of which make the commitments of full-time politics an almost impossible choice; women are under-represented in the jobs that most favour political careers; women are discouraged by the attentions of a hostile media; women are actively excluded by the male selectorates who guard the gateways to political life (Randall 1987). Within the general tendency to give due weight to each of these factors, there are still important variations in emphasis. Some writers have focused more on what stops women coming forward, and others on the male barriers when they nonetheless do (Lovenduski and Hills 1981 is an example of the latter). And some writers focus attention on political conditions, while others identify the social and economic obstacles to change.

In the more 'political' category are the arguments about proportional representation, which have been most associated in the British context (they are less of an issue elsewhere) with the work of Elizabeth Vallance (1979) and more recently Pippa Norris (1985). Single-member constituencies with a first-past-the-post system for selecting the winner are said to stack the cards in favour of the male, for in our sex-divided patriarchal societies, the man is the norm, the woman peculiar. If, on top of the relentless privileging of the male, the woman is less confident (and how extraordinary if she is not), the man has more political experience (all too likely if he never took time off from meetings to care for his children), or works in a job which has political links (trade union official, lawyer, journalist), why on earth should the woman come first? In a multi-member constituency the selectorate might take the risk – and indeed, when they are choosing not one but three or five candidates, it begins to look odd if they are all of them the same. In particular, where elections are organized through party lists there is considerably more scope for dictating sexual composition. It becomes possible to set a minimum quota for each sex in the winnable positions, or, even more ambitiously, to put men and women in alternate order on the list and produce parity in the final results. The evidence from Europe is not decisive but certainly suggestive. Those countries which rely on the single-member, first-past-the-post system have found it hardest to advance on the 5 per cent token representation. Most of those with a system of multi-member constituencies and party lists edge towards a 10 per cent representation of women. All those that stand out as spectacularly progressive employ proportional representation with party lists (Norris 1985; Lovenduski 1986; Haavio-Mannila et al. 1985).

General arguments for and against proportional representation establish the difficulties in saying what is most democratic. The single transferable vote system allows voters to indicate a hierarchy of preferences, and protects us against a situation in which party A wins with a minority of votes, when parties B and C are between them the first and second preferences of the majority. The implication, however, is that the party that ends up with most seats could be one that has fewer first preference votes – and if people really wanted their first choice, but only marginally preferred their second to their third, this could be a compromise that leaves the majority unhappy. The multi-member constituency can iron out some of the inequalities in first-past-the-post systems, but the smaller parties within each constituency may still end up with no members in parliament even if their support through the nation turned out quite impressive. The additional or mixed member system tries to deal with this by leaving some (usually half) seats selected on the first-past-the-post system, but distributing the remainder in proportion to the parties' share of the national vote. The problem here is that if the way we vote in our constituencies is still premised on our perception of which parties have the most chance in our area (we don't simply vote for what we most want, but for what we prefer given what we think others will do) then the figures for national voting cannot be presumed to reflect genuine preference. And, as opponents of any of these systems will argue, proportional representation can give undue influence to the small party that then holds the balance of power. Getting a 'fair' reflection of parties in parliament does not guarantee fair reflection in government.

In terms of the 'mirror' effect of reflecting the population, however, some form of proportional representation wins hands down over first-past-the-post systems (and when the New Zealand Commission on Electoral Reform recommended the abolition of Maori seats, it was with the proviso that the country should switch to a mixed member proportional system, thereby increasing Maori chances of election). In her study of 'Women's legislative participation in Western Europe' (1985) Pippa Norris compares twenty-four liberal democracies, including eighteen in Western Europe, to assess the correlation between the numbers of women elected and institutional, cultural and socioeconomic conditions. The institutional differences refer to the electoral system: whether the country operates a party list proportional system or some version of majoritarianism, including first-past-the-post, alternative vote and single transferable vote systems. Cultural differences were defined by the strength of Catholicism versus Protestantism (the former seen as more traditionalist for women), and with the help of data contributed by nine countries in the European Community in a survey on attitudes to sexual equality in politics. Socio-economic differences were roughly identified by the proportions of women in the labour force, their proportions in higher education and their proportions in the professions.

As in any cross-national survey, the measures are a bit rough and ready, but the results proved striking enough. Differences in electoral systems emerged as by far the most significant in relation to the election of women, followed at some distance by positions on the index of political egalitarianism. The dominant religion proved insignificant, as did socio-economic conditions. Among the notable individual examples, Switzerland is particularly convincing. Women were not granted full equal rights till 1971, and the society is so traditional in its views that as late as 1982 male citizens were still voting in one canton to deny women the vote in local elections. Swiss women nonetheless weigh in at over 10 per cent in the Nationalrat – under a system of proportional representation (Norris 1985:99).

Ten per cent is no great cause for rejoicing, and the fact that a particular electoral system can marginally enhance women's participation does not take us very far down the road. Looking beyond the clear evidence that proportional representation offers more favourable conditions for women to be elected, what dictates when real parity will be won? Is it a matter of women's political mobilization, both inside and outside of party politics, which can make sexual equality a question of public concern? Does it depend in any way on shifts in economic and social arrangements: an equalization in male and female rates of participation in the labour market? a desegregation in the jobs that men and women typically do? Is the heart of the matter the conditions under which children are cared for and reared, so that as long as this remains the private responsibility of invisible women, there is limited time for them to invade men's political sphere? Coming as I do from a tradition that has viewed political equalities as a reflex, however complicated and over-determined, of social and economic equalities, I thought for many years that a social revolution was the only real answer. As long as women are positioned as the dependants of men – a positioning which seems to rest on such an interlocking of social, economic and cultural forces that it is hard to know where to begin – it had seemed inconceivable to me that men and women could take equal parts in the political realm. Add on to this the more specifically feminist analysis of the relationship between public and private, which sees the determined amnesia over the domestic domain as central to liberal democracy, and the facts required no further explanation. What else could one possibly expect? What has shifted me towards the more political end of the spectrum – to the belief, that is, that greater political equality is possible even pending fundamental social transformation – is the recent experience of the Nordic countries.

Women in nordic countries Up till the 1960s there was not much to choose between any of the countries in Western or Northern Europe: a somewhat more damning obstructionism in first-past-the-post systems; a more conservative tendency where the church held its sway; generally just the deafening dominance of men. By 1984, however, women had taken 15 per cent of the parliamentary seats in Iceland, 26 per cent in Norway and Denmark, 28 per cent in Sweden and 31 per cent in Finland (Lovenduski 1986:152). In 1985, Norway took the world record. Women made up 34.4 per cent of the Storting (the national assembly), held eight out of eighteen cabinet posts, contributed 40.5 per cent of the membership of county councils and contributed 31.1 per cent of the membership of municipal councils. The relatively poor performance of women in Iceland further confirms the role played by electoral systems, for while Iceland shares with other Nordic countries the practice of proportional representation, the small number of constituencies combines with a large number of parties to mean that few parties can anticipate winning more than two seats in any one constituency. As in so many countries, women are typically nominated to the 'ornamental' positions on a party's list, with the first two places secured to men. Their position is thus more comparable to that in first-past-the-post systems (Skard and Haavio-Mannila 1985b).

Taking these countries as a whole, what is striking is that, despite significant economic differences with countries in Western Europe, the pattern of women's employment and the presumption of women's primary responsibilities for children are not so many miles away from the European norm. General economic conditions are certainly better, with much lower unemployment, much less of a gap between male and female hourly earnings, and much higher spending on social services. But the post-war growth in women's employment has, as in Britain and much of Europe, been largely a growth in part-time jobs for women (Finland is an exception here). The jobs women do are, as in Britain and elsewhere, typically at the lower paid, lower status end of the spectrum, with a familiar segregation into clerical work and public and private services. As Helga Maria Hernes notes in *Welfare State and Woman Power*, 'in all the Scandinavian countries, as in most industrialized societies, gender is the best predictor of a person's social status' (1987:28). State provision of childcare services is far superior but even so covers on average only one-third of preschool children, and much of it is still part-time provision, enabling women to work only in part-time jobs. In a recent discussion of sexual equality in the Nordic countries, Torild Skard and Elina Haavio-Manilla (1986) argue that 'one of the most pressing problems is the lack of child-care facilities': a comment that is all too familiar to women elsewhere. The social position of women is still informed by the statistically anachronistic but nonetheless powerful assumption that men occupy the world of work and women the world of the home.

The contrasts seem puzzling indeed. In 1988 I attended a forum that brought together feminists from Western and Northern Europe, centring much of its discussion around the impact of quota systems in increasing the political profile of women. The women from West Germany were still digesting the causes and consequences of the recent conference decision of the German Social Democratic Party (SPD), which just that year had committed itself to a minimum of 25 per cent women among its Bundestag members at the next election, progressing to a minimum of 40 per cent in the course of the next ten years. Feminists from Britain could hardly begin to conceive the conditions under which comparable decisions might be reached in Britain. By contrast, those from Norway or Sweden had experienced quota systems for so long that they could barely remember when they won this battle – or indeed if it was a battle at all!

The pattern, in fact, was as follows. In the 1970s a number of Scandinavian parties adopted the principle of at least 40 per cent female representation at all levels of elected delegation within the party itself. This was adopted by the Swedish Liberal Party and the Swedish Communist Party in 1972, by the Norwegian Liberal Party in 1974 and the Norwegian Socialist Left Party in 1975, and by the Danish Socialist People's Party in 1977 (Skard and Haavio-Mannila 1985a). In the 1980s there was a push to extend this to the level of female representation in national parliaments. In 1980, parties in both Norway and Sweden proposed legislation that would commit *all* political parties to a minimum of 40 per cent women on their electoral lists; failing the success of this bid, various parties introduced the practice unilaterally (Skard and Haavio-Mannila 1985b). In 1983, for example, the Norwegian Labour Party introduced a 40 per cent quota for candidates in local and national elections and, as the largest party after the 1985 elections, contributed significantly to the lead that Norway then assumed. Among the parties that remain ideologically opposed to the principle of a quota system, there has also been substantial movement: the Norwegian Conservative Party espouses 'competence' in opposition to formal quotas, but women nonetheless make up 30 per cent of its current national representation (Skjeie 1988). Again this seems to confirm the importance of specifically political factors. Once a few parties have put their toes in the water, the exigencies of competition require that the others do not lag too far behind.

The initial moves towards increasing women's representation pre-dated – or at the latest coincided with – the emergence of the contemporary women's movement; indeed, with the exception of Denmark and to a lesser extent Iceland, the Nordic countries were rather slow to develop the characteristically counter-cultural politics of second wave feminism. This itself is rather daunting in its implications. Through most of Europe, the women's movement showed little enthusiasm for the conventionalities of representative democracy, and it was not till quite late in the 1970s that feminists began to look to existing political parties as an important arena for change. Many parties had their own women's organizations, often dating from the late nineteenth century when women members were mobilized to perform various supportive or fund-raising activities. At key periods, these women's sections had worked hard to raise feminist issues, but this early history was lost to most of the activists in the new women's movement; outside of the Nordic countries, connections were rarely made.

Yet in Sweden, Norway and Finland, it was the women's sections in the social democratic parties that began to make the running, and in a chronology that has no parallel in the rest of Europe, it is the 1950s that are described as the 'decade of the build-up' and the 1960s as the 'explosive decade' (Eduards et al. 1985:136). A wide-ranging debate on sex roles in society, including Alva Myrdal and Viola Klein's *Women's Two Roles*, made the status of women an early matter of public concern. Long before such issues entered the public agenda elsewhere, the Nordic countries were setting up official commissions on equality issues:

1960 in Sweden, 1963 in Finland, 1964 in Norway and 1965 in Denmark (Eduards et al. 1985).

Nordic writers have commented that their countries exhibit a passion for equality (see the book with this title, edited by Graubard, 1986), though many also reflect a troubled appreciation that the worship of mediocrity can appear as its more negative side. 'Fifty years ago,' writes Hans Fredrik Dahl, 'Aksel Sandemose formulated an ironic code for Nordic behaviour called "the Law of Jante", in which were reflected all the dark sides of small-scale societies insisting on equity: envy, jealousy, and extreme degrees of social control' (in Graubard 1986:108). As the comment indicates, this ruling egalitarianism has been partially attributed to the small scale of Nordic societies – with populations ranging from 200,000 in Iceland to eight million in Sweden – and the associated homogeneity. Norway, Finland and Iceland were additionally subjected to foreign rule and thereby 'saved' from a powerful indigenous aristocracy, but since the dominant countries (Denmark and Sweden) share much the same political culture as those dominated, this cannot be considered a full explanation. It has been further argued that the often sparsely distributed populations generate a preference for single-track solutions – a single university system, a single broadcasting company, a single school system – and though the multiplicity of political parties might seem an exception to this, it is notable that party allegiances have been divided less definitively along the fault lines of class than in many other countries.

Whatever the validity of these analyses, there is no guarantee that a general egalitarianism will translate into sexual egalitarianism – and if the Nordic passion for equality is indeed bound up with a 'small town' mentality, one might anticipate on the contrary a conservative attitude towards women. The explanations offered by Nordic feminists have therefore focused more closely on the nature of the public/private divide and suggest contrasts between liberal and social democracy. Two key points emerge from these discussions. The first is that post-war social democracies in Scandinavia assumed considerably more responsibilities not only for welfare provision (more spending on social services than in other parts of Europe) but perhaps as importantly for welfare policy. All contemporary states have an agenda for women and the family, but it is often covert and contradictory, and hard to expose to the public gaze. In the Nordic countries, the state took on itself a more explicitly interventionist role in forming and transforming what in other countries have been regarded as pre-eminently private affairs.

Thus Helga Maria Hernes talks of the 'mutual permeability of state, market, family, and public sphere' (1988:209) and the ways in which this shifted the division between public and private, personal and communal, making women 'objects' of public policy in a much more visible way. The argument is not that this automatically favoured women, or that of itself it ensured to women a more active role. The first policies on women's status came, she argues, from paternalism rather than women's own participation. 'Women were the objects of policy long before they ever became subjects in the political process' (1987:27). But the explicit association between women and public policy had its effect. It eventually mobilized women on a broader platform than that offered by the women's movement and legitimized their concerns as being a part of what politics is about.

The other aspect to this was the growth of corporate structures in the Nordic countries, seen by some women as playing an ambiguous but in the end progressive role. Until recently, women were grossly under-represented in the plethora of public councils, boards and committees that operate as the extended arm of the Nordic state and play an increasingly dominant role in formulating government policy. Members are largely nominated on to these bodies by ministries (that is, not even by the parties in government) and have been drawn primarily from those considered 'experts' (civil servants and academics) and from the key economic interest groups (associations of workers and employers). The corporate system initially worked against women's participation; to the extent that it offered any kind of democratization, the beneficiaries were from the male working class. Indeed much of the discussion over women's improved profile in parliamentary politics has centred around the pessimistic thesis that women were let in only when the men had lost interest (Holter 1984). Corporatism undermined the powers of parliament, reserving to these nominated bodies much of the crucial policy process, and it was at that point, not before, that parliament became more open to women. Just as women have been allowed slightly more access to local government because the peripheries have less power than the centre, so women have been permitted to take their seats in parliament because the real power has shifted elsewhere.

But as more of the key economic issues were debated and

effectively decided outside of parliament, party politicians began to turn to 'women's concerns' as one of the few areas in which it was possible to establish some identity or role (Eduards et al. 1985). More time became available to debate such issues and, against the deadening weight of inter-party consensus on economic affairs, these more 'domestic' matters became a way of securing some continuing profile. These then entered into the corporate structure itself. Equal Status Councils were set up at national level in 1972 in Norway, Finland and Sweden, in 1975 in Denmark and in 1976 in Iceland; over the same period Equal Status Committees were formed at local government level, particularly in Norway. The relatively high visibility for issues of sexual equality has in the end backfired on the corporate system; in 1973 Norway led the way in insisting that all agencies nominating candidates to public boards or committees must include some women as well as men. The overall shift in corporate membership is not yet impressive, but certainly suggests that this, too, is becoming more accessible to women (see table).

That women are now permeating the corporate structures undermines the cynical view that their high profile in local and national politics is merely a function of these latter losing their power. The thesis is also challenged from its other direction by Hege Skjeie, who notes that there is no conclusive evidence that the traditional sphere of politics is less influential in Nordic countries than elsewhere, and indeed some counter-evidence from Norway that parliament has still held on to its power (1988:18–20).

The remarkable levels of female participation in these countries can I think be explained by a combination of three factors. The first is the enabling condition of their systems of proportional representation, which opens up but does not guarantee more space. The second is the strength of women's organizations within the

Table 3.1   Proportion of women on public boards, councils, committees in Nordic countries (%)

	Denmark	Finland	Iceland	Norway	Sweden
1972	8	11	3	10	7
1979	8	7	6	20	16
1985	15	13	n.a	30	17

Source: Hernes 1987:98.

traditional social democratic parties, and the political choices made by feminists who have attached greater significance to conventional power. The third is the differences between liberal and social democracy, which hinge around a different relationship between public and private spheres; women's position has been made a more explicit public concern. Each of these begs questions about what explains them in turn, but they combine to highlight the importance of *politics*, and the scope for specifically political change.

This does not mean the road is now clear. We can draw some reassurance from the effects of example and competition and anticipate that the process will speed up once the first stages are won. But repeating the experience of one country in another is not easy, and when Pippa Norris identified the importance of proportional representation she found herself correspondingly depressed. 'Given the many institutional barriers to political equality, including a resistance to the implementation of electoral reform in majoritarian systems, it seems unlikely that cross-national diffences in the political position of women will diminish in the near future' (1985:100). All the trends seem to suggest a continuing growth in female participation in wage employment, higher education and the professions. By early 1989, even the Conservative Government in Britain had woken up to the anticipated shortages of skilled labour and burst forth in a series of unlikely pronouncements on the desirability of increasing the proportion of women in higher education, of establishing workplace nurseries (not of course financed by the state), and encouraging more women to work. But if the entry of women into higher education and paid employment has limited impact on their numbers in elected office (as the example of the United States reveals all too clearly), none of these changes can be expected to make much difference. It is crass materialism to say that what is 'only' political is therefore more open to change. On the other hand, if it *is* a matter of politics we do at least know where to begin.

With all its limitations, representative democracy is not necessarily inimical to the election of women, and indeed gender may now prove less intransigent than class. I do not hold out great hopes for my own country, but find it entirely plausible that liberal and, more specifically, social democracies will witness a growing proportion of women in politics, even pending that social revolution I once thought a necessary condition. But those elected will be peculiarly skewed to a certain kind of woman who, like the generations of men who went before her, will be a well-educated professional, and devoted to politics full time. Even in the Nordic countries, the marked shifts of recent years do not guarantee access for all women, any more than previous patterns of elected and corporate representation guaranteed access for all men. The women elected to parliament may be thoroughly 'unrepresenta-tive' in terms of their class, their income, the number and age of their children, or whether they previously worked full or part-time. The fact that gender quotas are increasingly accepted is no doubt a reflection of this: with women distributed (however unevenly) across the range of occupations and professions, they can be incorporated into our representative assemblies without disturbing the conventions of competence and leadership, and without disrupting the dominance of class. However distant the prospect of a gender quota may seem to feminists in Britain or the United States, it is at least conceivable. No one even talks of a formal quota for class.

Representative democracy may prove itself more amenable than I once thought to the election of women, but it has trouble with their 'representation'. Grounded as it is in a tradition that rests on the abstract individual, liberal/representative democracy has to define politics as the realm of public rationality in which we contest opposing ideas. The least democratic versions of this will leave the bulk of issues to be settled by those elected, and the electorate as a whole will be permitted to make its occasional foray into the voting booth only to indicate a preference over who these people should be. More radical versions will try to commit the representatives to an explicitly delineated set of policies and ideas, so that we will not only be able to 'punish' those who disappoint us by not voting for them the next time round, but can more positively influence the decisions they make. Here the emphasis will be on party congresses, definite commitments, explicit propo-sals, a heightened profile for ideas.

The representation of women *as women* potentially founders on both the difficulties of defining the shared interests of women and the difficulties of establishing mechanisms through which these interests are voiced. It has been noted that women politicians are often reluctant to see themselves as representing women. While we may regret this refusal of feminist concerns, we cannot jump straight to the opposite camp. Feminism should not give unwitting support to a version of democracy that rests too exclusively on trust, as if merely by virtue of their sex women can presume a mandate to speak for us all. The representation of women as women does not fit within the framework of representative democracy, and while this may count as ammunition in the battle for democracy of a different kind, it should not be glossed over in discussions of change.

4

PUBLIC SPACES, PRIVATE LIVES

The representation of women is about who gets elected, and even in the most optimistic scenarios it still deals with a political elite. This does not stop it mattering, but for the majority of feminists the questions of democracy have been wider in scope, revolving around prior issues of what 'politics' and 'political' should mean. The significance feminism attaches to the distinctions between public and private should by now be clear, for the boundary (if any) is continually contested, and most have argued that the relationship must be redefined. To put it with rather more dramatic panache, the women's movement has claimed that 'the personal is political'. As Iris Young notes, the women's movement 'has made public issues out of many practices claimed too trivial or private for public discussion: the meaning of pronouns, domestic violence against women, the practice of men's opening doors for women, the sexual assault on women and children, the sexual division of housework and so on' (1987:74). Things that used to be dismissed as trivial can no longer be viewed as the haphazard consequence of individual choice, for they are structured by relations of power. Things once shrouded in the secrecies of private existence are and should be of public concern. The sexual division of labour and the sexual distribution of power are as much part of politics as relations between classes or negotiations between nations, and what goes on in the kitchen and bedroom cries out for political change.

The conventional distinction between public and private conjures up an image of the public as occupying a specific place: the grandiose chambers of the national assembly; the scaled-down versions of the local town hall. And while political scientists have occasionally played with the idea that politics exists wherever there is conflict – a more expansive notion that could accommodate some women's movement concerns – most fall back into circularity. Politics is about public decisions, and it occurs in a public space. It refers to ministers and cabinets, parliaments and councils; it means parties and pressure groups, civil service and courts. Under the rubric of public opinion, the concept can stretch itself to take on the media, political culture, the schools. But politics is not a question of who looks after the children and who goes out to work, or of who addresses the meeting and who makes the tea. These are private affairs.

It is a measure of the changes that feminism has helped bring about that my contrast already sounds forced, and if I am re-erecting some ancient monument just in order to tear it down. The competing notion that everything is political also has wide currency today (perhaps the noun still attaches itself to definite places, while the adjective will go any old where?). Though the women's movement has no copyright on this, it can certainly claim some credit for spreading the idea around. This is the more extraordinary when we consider the context out of which 'the personal is political' came.

It was initially a riposte to male politicos in the civil rights and socialist/radical movements: activists whose conception of politics was far too grand to admit the pertinence of merely sexual concerns. From the middle of the 1960s, women in a number of advanced capitalist countries (though most markedly in the USA) were beginning to question their treatment in Left organizations. The men made the decisions while the women typed the leaflets, and despite the supposed joint commitment to liberating the world, the women were still regarded as just a good time in bed. As David Bouchier has noted, the phrase 'women's liberation' was first adopted (round about 1964) with mildly satirical intent (1983: 52). Liberation was the word of the moment, and in applying to themselves a term usually reserved for heroic peoples struggling against imperialist aggression, women hoped to establish parallels that no good militant could deny.

Deny it they did, amid gales of laughter and patronizing sneers, and it was against this background that women so much needed to claim their concerns as 'political'. (The context is revealing, for who else except dedicated radicals would have thought political the thing to be?) A lengthier version of the slogan dating from a 1967 women's newsletter helps fill in the details. After a major conference on the so-called New Politics which had brought together various Left groups but denied any platform to women, Chicago feminists launched the *Voice of the Women's Liberation Movement*. Attacking the blinkered horizons of their erstwhile comrades, they announced that 'the liberation of women from their oppression is a problem as worthy of political struggle as any other that the New Politicians were considering' (cited in Bouchier 1983:53). Women's problems are political too.

The 'political' to which these women were laying claim was not the world of elections or governments or theories of the state. Politics worked as shorthand for all those structures (in the language of the time, this would be institutions) of exploitation and oppression against which struggle must be waged. In describing the personal as political, women were contesting those activists who had sneered at their 'trivial' concerns. It *did* matter that women were treated as sexual objects to be consumed by the more powerful men. It *did* matter that wives had to pander to their husbands because they could not earn enough to live on their own. It *did* matter that organizations whose rhetoric leapt from one grand proclamation of freedom to another still refused to consider the inequalities of women. Men had power over women, and where there was oppression, there politics came in.

Beyond its early history in 1960s radicalism, the personal is political came to assume a whole complex of meanings. In its most combative forms it dissolved all distinction between public and private, personal and political, and came to regard all aspects of social existence as if they were an undifferentiated expression of male power. This was the version most associated with radical feminism, where patriarchal power came to be viewed as the primary form of oppression (either *the* primary or at least of equal status with class), and the hitherto private sphere of reproduction was identified as the site of this power. Politics and power then came to mean almost the same thing. In *Sexual Politics* (1970), for example, Kate Millett defined power as the essence of politics and patriarchal government as 'the institution whereby that half of the populace which is female is controlled by the half which is male' (p. 25). Though she refers to an institution, it is not one located in a particular place – we are a long way here from any conventional institutions of power.

For other feminists, this was a fearful collapse of public and private. Deploying 'the personal is political' to more sober effect, they used it to claim not identity but rather a relationship between two spheres. The key point here was that public and private cannot be dealt with as separate worlds, as if the one exists in a rhythm independent from the other. Thus relations inside family and household are knocked into the appropriate shape by a battery of public policies (on housing, for example, social security, education); conversely, relations at the workplace and in politics are moulded by the inequalities of sexual power. From this perspective, it is a nonsense to think of the 'personal' as something outside of politics, or to conceive of politics as immune to sexuality and 'private' concerns. And when the distinction is employed to deny social responsibility for what goes on behind so-called private doors, it is not only nonsense but directly oppressive.

Various inflections can be put on 'the personal is political', and each has implications for the way democracy is conceived. At its minimum, new topics are being placed on the political agenda, and in many cases this redefinition of what counts as public concerns has transformed the opportunities for women to become politically active. The politics that once seemed defined by alien abstractions has been reshaped to include the texture of daily life, offering what was to many a first opening into 'political' debate. When feminism turned its spotlight on family and household, it queried the places within which politics occurs, extending the demand for democracy to cover many more arenas. As Sheila Rowbotham has noted, feminism shifts attention towards the sphere of everyday life and widens the meaning of democracy 'to include domestic inequality, identity, control over sexuality, challenge to cultural representation, community control over state welfare and more equal access to public resources' (1986:85–6). When politics is redefined, so too is democracy.

But to say that feminism questions, transforms and in some instances dissolves the relationship between public and private is to beg rather a lot of questions. In assessing the implications for the theory and practice of democracy we need to consider which variant is involved. In her recent book on the British women's movement, Sheila Rowbotham notes that 'the personal is political' seemed to pop up in virtually every chapter, proving a more pervasive theme than she had expected to find (1989:295). The very range of associations gives a nightmarish quality to the phrase, particularly if you compound this (as I have chosen to do) by taking it to cover the same spectrum of possibilities as the more theoretically phrased 'we must rethink the relationship between public and private'.

Refashioning this relationship is so much at the heart of feminist politics that you could almost define the tradition in these terms. But so far I have used the phrase somewhat loosely, and mostly in discussing other traditions. I want now to examine the variety of ways in which feminists have queried the division into public and private spheres – and what I shall take to cover similar ground, the different meanings they have attached to the slogan that 'the personal is political'. I have separated out those aspects that have particular bearing on the problems of democracy, different inflections that may not have equal weight in feminist theory or practice but are the most pertinent in this context. To those who have lived through the last two decades of the women's movement, my emphasis may seem eccentric, or even to miss the point, for while some of what I say will be instantly recognizable as part of the politics of the last twenty years, the rest is phrased in terms that derive from other traditions. The relevance will nonetheless emerge.

Private constraints on public involvement The first aspect already appears in chapter 2 and is the one that will come easiest to those versed in mainstream democratic debate. It links the feminist imperative on the relationship between public and private to existing arguments about the degrees of control people exert through their working lives. In this version, 'the personal is political' draws attention to the dependence of one sphere on the other, noting that democracy in the home is a precondition for democracy abroad. Supporters of participatory democracy have told us that the experience of hierarchy and subordination at work undercuts our equal development as citizens. If this is so, how much more so does the experience of subordination and submission at home?

Feminists have explored two aspects here, one of them brutally practical and the other to do with our identity and sense of our selves. In the first place women are prevented from participating in public life because of the way their private lives are run. The division of labour between women and men constitutes for most women a double burden of work. In the advanced capitalist countries, the proportion of women working in paid employment (whether in full-time or part-time jobs) has continued to rise throughout the last three decades; in the socialist bloc countries, women have long played a major role in the full-time labour force;

in the newly industrializing countries, women provide much of the labour for the textile, electronics and computer components factories; and in those countries in which agriculture is still the main source of employment, women continue to play a major (often the major) role in farming the land. In all cases, women also retain primary responsibility for children and household.

The mere pressures of time will keep most women out of any of the processes of decision-making on offer. The active citizenry of the ancient world was freed for participation in public affairs by a vast army of women and slaves who performed the necessary household labour. Today, the most foolhardy of democrats would not risk resurrecting that ideal, for given the contemporary equation of democracy with equality, we must all be more modest in our ideas of what active citizenship entails. But the way our private lives are organized promotes male involvement and reduces female participation. Who collects the children and who makes the tea is a vital political concern.

Often more numbing than the sheer accumulation of practical obstacles is the different experience men and women have of power. Women have only to walk down the street to be reminded of their physical vulnerability and lack of social power, and the night-time scurry from one lighted area to another does not enhance one's feelings of confidence or control. Inside each household there may be too much variation by class, region, race or religion to hazard a generalization over who takes the major family decisions – but the men earn more money and all too often they abuse their greater physical power. Most women's experience at work certainly fits the routinized pattern that has been identified by advocates of workplace democracy as destroying any sense of efficacy or control, while the dominance of nature in women's home lives (by which I mean both the grander experiences of pregnancy and childbirth and the more mundane level of feeding and washing and changing the nappies) does not encourage women to believe they can reshape their world.

This is one aspect of the relationship between public and private spheres, and part of what feminists have meant in claiming the personal as political can be read along these lines. Every study of women's involvement in trade unions ends with necessary if monotonous regularity by recommending that union meetings should be held in work hours, for women need their lunch breaks to do the shopping and often have to dash off after work to collect the children and make the tea. The women's movement has established the practice of organizing creches at conferences, and has had some considerable success in persuading other groups to acknowledge this need. Confronted with hostile questions as to why women need to meet in isolation from men, feminists have frequently argued that the experience of domestic and familial subservience undermines women's self-confidence, and that the patterns of male dominance will continue to reassert themselves until women have learnt to participate in groups of their own. In each instance, the current organization of 'private' life is being presented as a major obstacle to the democratic involvement of women. If democracy were just about the occasional trip out to vote, then the differences might not much matter. But as soon as you move on to a more participatory notion of democracy, then equal involvement of women and men seems to depend on substantial change in the private sphere.

It is I think a measure of the close analogy between this and the longer standing arguments for participatory democracy that the handful of men who have taken up the relationship between feminism and democracy have often concentrated their energies here. David Held, for example, writes in 'collective responsibility for mundane tasks and reduction of routine labour to a minimum' (1986:291) as one of the conditions for his preferred model of democratic autonomy, and clearly has the experience of women in mind. The fullest discussion I know comes in Philip Green's *Retrieving Democracy* (1985a), which works within a tradition of radical democracy that has focused on the enabling conditions outside of the conventionally 'political' sphere (significantly enough, the subtitle of his book is In Search of Civic Equality, and his central argument is that substantial social equality is the precondition for significant political democracy). Green argues that the division between mental and manual labour which is characteristic of capitalist societies is such that it denies a majority of citizens the chance to develop their capabilities and contributes to a kind of pseudodemocracy in which political influence, access or participation is for most people 'an episodic and occasional or even nonexistent event' (p. 179).

Unlike the typical supporter of participatory democracy, he does not attach much weight to workplace democracy, nor does he insist on the absolute social equality that more romantic socialists espouse. His programme revolves around a democratic division of labour that would abolish *permanent* hierarchies in production – and in an explicit discussion of how this relates to women, he extends it to include a democratic division of labour in reproduction. A lifetime's access to education and training figures largely in this vision; shared parenting, combined with greater social support to those with young children, are the crucial additions that will get women included as well. Each individual must be genuinely – not just formally – free to change his or her position in life, and only with this substantive job mobility can we begin to talk of citizens being equal. Social equality thus 'means that we are never able to say of anyone: he or she is statistically unlikely to ever exercise public responsibility merely because of the possession of some social attribute: being poor or a factory worker or a member of a racial or ethnic subculture, or a female, etc.' (Green 1985a:170).

Every feminist who has written on women and politics makes some similar point. Even in the least demanding task of political participation (slipping down the road to vote), women fell for many years behind men, and surveys indicate that this combined with a lesser sense of involvement, knowledge and competence in the 'outside' political world (see, for instance, Lovenduski 1986: ch. 4). The gap in voter turnout has since closed and 'in Western democracies it has frequently diminished to negligible proportions or disappeared outright' (Randall 1987:53). But on most other indices of political participation, women participate less then men. One possible and, if so, significant exception is what Vicky Randall calls women's *ad hoc* participation 'in political campaigns that are relatively short-lived, throwing up makeshift organizations and tending to rely on direct tactics such as pickets, squats and self-help projects. Typically too, they focus on issues of local or community concern' (p. 58). Though the evidence is patchy, it points to a substantial female presence here – in a politics around housing, childcare, transport or the environment, all, of course, issues of direct family or household concern. Sex remains a significant (though not the most significant) indicator of where and how much we are politically involved, and the conventions that have assigned women a primary responsibility in the domestic sphere are a major component in this.

On this issue, I consider the argument won almost as soon as it stated, and the many centuries through which no one made the connection testify only to the vigour with which women were concealed. Political equality between women and men must include substantial changes in the domestic sphere: an equalization, for example, of the hours we work; a shift in the responsibilities that women shoulder for housework and children; a break in the patterns that divide men and women so unequally between work in the home and work outside. Whether at the simplest level of having no free time, or as a more complex consequence of always being told what to do, women's experiences in the home continually undercut the possibilities for democracy.

The more difficult point to establish is exactly how much this matters. Just as with the relationship between being pushed around at work and becoming convinced that politics is something for others, there has to be *some* connection. But if the stakes are raised till transforming the sexual division of labour in the household becomes the single most important precondition for political equality, then the association becomes less clear. My own arguments in chapter 3, for example, suggest that at the level of local councils and national assemblies, the sexual division of labour may not be decisive in determining women's participation. There is certainly a link between the proportion of women elected as representatives and the kind of economic and social policies that a country has pursued; but there is greater variation between countries than could be anticipated from differences in women's position in the labour market or in the availability of support services for children. We could not claim that the countries where women are edging up towards 40 per cent participation in national politics have experienced a 'democratization of the division of labour in reproduction', and if we tried to do so, local feminists would soon set us right. But if the marked increases in women's representation have a largely political explanation, maybe it does not so much matter whether men share the childcare, or nursery provision is improved?

The point is that it may not much matter if what is at issue is the equalization of men and women in the national legislature or local or state government. If they are only given the chance, there will always be a pool of women who make themselves available for election, some by extraordinary efforts of combining politics and children and work, others by remaining childless, others by having well-paid jobs and being able to purchase domestic help. But if democracy is to mean more than the opportunity to vote in periodic elections and the equal right to stand as candidates, it has to involve a more substantial degree of participation, and more genuine openness, regardless of sex, race or class. We might hesitate before the kind of mean-spirited hypothetical that permits only one choice for change, but equalizing the distribution of responsibilities and time in each household will surely figure as a candidate on the list. If men and women are to be political equals in any more substantial sense than the equal right to vote, then this *is* a key condition.

This is part then of what feminism has to contribute to the debates on democracy: the importance of transforming the familial, domestic, 'private' sphere; of laying the groundwork for a democratic society by democratizing sexual relations in the home. But the arguments so far follow a well-worn track, extending established connections between social and political life. Equality in the household is being presented as a means to an end, as a necessary condition for what we really want, which is democracy in the wider sphere. To this extent, the argument does not capture the full flavour of 'the personal is political'. Taking an analogy from more general debates between socialists and feminists, it is as if the equality of the sexes is being promoted because it has been discovered that it contributes to the development of socialism, but is not valued as an end in itself. Yet the personal is political has usually meant more than that the personal *affects* the political; even in its most sober guises, it is saying that the personal is political too. The second meaning attached to the slogan is thus one that stresses the ubiquity of power. Never mind the learning process, never mind the equalization of time, never mind cumulative effects of household equality on political participation outside. Democracy is *as* important in the household as anywhere else, for in the household there is unequal power.

Power as all-pervasive It is frequently noted that each new wave of feminism has to rediscover what previous generations found out, and that, in a pattern that seems to bury all the earlier contributions, each period thinks itself unique. Bearing this in mind, I will nonetheless hazard a comment. When the women's movement re-emerged in the late 1960s, it was particularly insistent on women's unhappiness in the family – through boredom, lack of control and because of violence. While the external world of jobs and pay and media and politics figured significantly in campaigns and on the agenda of demands, the more burning preoccupations were often closer to home. In the consciousness-raising groups that were so vital in this period, women began to grapple with their sense of identity and frustration, and, as Sheila Rowbotham describes in her account of the British movement, moved from a puzzled indictment of men's emotional incapacity and women's emotional dependence to a starker sense of coercion and control (1989:6–10). Men and women were supposed to be related through love, but sexuality seemed to be distorting our relations with those who were not our lovers and bringing vulnerability and pain with those who were. Heterosexual love began to look like a trap. Stripped of its romantic gloss, the family began to emerge as a site of male power, a power that in its more benign aspects got women working excessively long hours for minimal reward, and in its worst could expose them to physical and sexual abuse. The family was no haven in a heartless world, the lover no guarantee of harmony or bliss.

This harsher view of family and sexual relations carried with it a more pervasive definition of power. Many had thought of problems they had with husbands or lovers in terms of individual psychology – maybe we're not compatible? maybe I want what's impossible? maybe he just doesn't care? – but in the process of exploring individual experiences, they came to identify general patterns of power. Feminists then disagreed profoundly over who was responsible (was it men or capitalism or structures or roles?) but were reasonably united in stressing the subordination of women in the home. In relation to democracy, this implied a good deal more than the idea that equality in the household is a condition for democracy in the state. It was not just that women were prevented from participating in external activities by the pressures and constraints of the home; women's impotence and subordination, their submission and dependence, crucially mattered in themselves. The personal was *as* political as anything else, and as devastatingly destructive of our human development as anything that governments could do.

This broader conception of power has been cited as one of feminism's major innovations, and those theorists who have focused attention on the different spaces within which democracy is required often make their bow towards women for their help in changing the agenda. Samuel Bowles and Herbert Gintis, for example, commend the women's movement for identifying the heterogeneity of power and for reminding us that domination is no respecter of place. Placing it in the broad tradition of 'radical democracy' in which they locate themselves, they link it with a rather ragbag assortment of deviants: 'the seventeenth-century leveller, the nineteenth-century chartists and agrarian populists, and the twentieth-century feminists and advocates of worker councils' (1986:8). All these, they argue, have conceived of politics as a matter of 'becoming', as something which cannot be reduced to a bid for resources but which involves transforming the very interests it pursues. The other common denominator is that all have viewed oppression as multi-layered, spanning the family, economy and state. For Bowles and Gintis, there will be many arenas in which democracy is vital. Concentrating on contemporary Western societies, they select out three crucial sites: the liberal democratic state, the capitalist economy, and the patriarchal family. The issue of domination arises wherever there is a 'socially consequential yet democratically unaccountable power' (p. 101); where these two come together, there is a case for democratization.

All this makes it sound a good deal simpler than it is and leaves us with some uneasy questions about the differences between democratizing the family, household or community, democratizing the workplace, and democratizing the state. The democratization of the workplace, for example, can occur through state intervention, through legislation that requires firms to set up decision-making structures that will involve employees or their representatives, that dictates the nature and range of decisions that must be put to the employees, or, more ambitiously, that enforces a transfer of ownership to the workers. The 'democratization of everyday life' is not open to the same kind of process. We can perhaps imagine the kind of decision-making structures that would equalize power within the household, but would we welcome the household inspectorate whose job it might be to enforce them? In the first case, we can regulate for democracy. In the second, we are calling on participants to take democracy into their own hands. It is one thing to say that both spheres are characterized by democratically unaccountable power, but once we turn to what might be the democratic solutions, there are important distinctions of kind.

Among critics of contemporary feminism the main distinction is to do with scale of significance, and the questions are designed with bathetic intent. How can equalizing the decisions over who changes the nappies be comparable with equal rights to vote? This is a game that anyone can play, and the more fruitful line of enquiry is whether an over-assimilation of the personal and political endangers what is positive about private life. Carole Pateman signalled an early qualification when she noted that 'the interdependence of the personal and the political can be recognized, as can the fact that any relationship can, in certain circumstances, have political effects, but this is not the same as arguing that the criteria and principles that should order our interactions and decision-making as citizens should be exactly the same as those that should underlay our relationships with friends and lovers' (1975:467). More polemically and critically, Jean Bethke Elshtain has presented 'the personal is political' as an outrageous slogan of radical feminism and one that teems with totalitarian intent. 'Note,' she says, 'that the claim is not that the personal and political are interrelated in important and fascinating ways previously hidden to us by sexist ideology and practice; nor that the personal and the political may be analogous to one another along certain axes of power and privilege, but that the personal *is* political' (1981:217). This simple equation, she argues, denies what are important distinctions between one kind of activity and another and blurs everything into ramifications of the same masculine power. 'The social world, from top to bottom, is one long, unmediated conduit permeated throughout by male oppression of the female, whether the male is defined as a natural aggressor, a demon, a member of the universal male sex-class, or a simple oppressor who throughout history has taken advantage of his superior physical strength' (p. 212). Public and private are collapsed into one, leaving no area of human existence that is deemed to exist outside of politics and no exemptions from political control.

Elshtain argues this in the context of a sustained critique of existing divisions between public and private, and in particular of the way that liberalism recast these as determinedly separate spheres. The result, she suggests, was disastrous. Into the public sphere went all the rationality of prudential calculation; while the private soaked up the sentimental remains. The conceptual links between politics and the familial were severed, and politics became defined as the most crass individualism, something that began and ended 'with mobilization of resources, achieving maximum impacts, calculating prudentially, articulating interest group claims, engaging in reward distribution functions' (Elshtain 1981:246). The heart went out of politics. The triumph of individualism emptied the public sphere of most of what politics should be about, while the pressure to extend individualist or contractarian principles into the innermost chambers of the private sphere threatens what deeper humanity still remains. This, she believes, is where the dangers of radical feminism come in, for in its simple equations of personal and political, it encourages the very worst tendencies in the modern world.

As many of her feminist critics have noted, Elshtain retains a sanguine view of the family (see, for example, Ehrenreich 1983; Siltanen and Stanworth 1984; Stacey 1986). 'I begin', she says in *Public Man, Private Woman*, 'with an affirmation: familial ties and modes of child-rearing are essential to establish the minimal foundations of human, social existence' (1981:326). Collective forms of childcare are said to sacrifice the child to the career of the mother and, while she indicates some sympathy with current notions of shared parenting, she gives no attention to any mechanisms that might bring this about. If feminists go down the 'me too' road of selfish rights and interests (dumping their children in institutionalized care, making a child's life a misery by squabbling with the father over who does most work) then instead of providing us with an alternative vision of society, they will be capitulating to the very forces that limit and coarsen our life.

Jean Bethke Elshtain's argument barely engages with the difficult conditions in which many children grow up: the resentments and depressions of isolated mothers; the enveloping swathes of a maternal love that can find no other object; the absence or indifference of too many fathers; the poverty of families living on only one income. I can think of few feminists who claim to have found the answer, but this hardly justifies giving up on the question. As Judith Stacey notes, 'Elshstain appears uninterested in, even hostile to, the subject of male domination . . . She rarely seems to comprehend what all the feminist fuss is about' (1986:232). The family is equated with the private, and the private with personal life, and in her main point of contact with classical liberalism (which otherwise is an object of critique), Elshtain seeks to defend this private world from the excesses of politicization.

Her own version of the distinction between public and private rests on a notion of *activities* that are different. It is not that politics exists 'out there' in a recognizable space of its own, but that some things we do are political and other things we do are not. If we drift into thinking that everything in our lives is a political problem, then we lay ourselves open to thinking everything has a political solution. 'Part of the struggle', she observes, 'involves reflecting on whether our current misery and unhappiness derive entirely from faulty and exploitative social forms that can, and therefore must, be changed or whether a large part of that unhappiness derives from the simple fact of being human, therefore limited, knowing that one is going to die' (Elshtain 1981:301). This kind of comment can always be a recipe for complacency, and

Elshtain's defence of the family can be faulted along such lines. As long as the seemingly intimate relations between men and women (or parents and children) are structured by state regulation, economic conditions and patriarchal power, then these relations are already politicized whether we want it or no. Elshtain's warning therefore carries only a residual weight. Difficult as it is to know where to draw the distinction (is poverty just part of being human? is frustration just evidence that we want too much?), there will be some things in life that must be left up to us, either to change, or simply accept. If we treat the personal as thoroughly identical to the political, we run the twin risks of believing our lives can be made perfect (with all the associated unhappiness when the belief proves ill-founded) and of handing over to others the responsibility for making them so.

A woman's right to choose Jean Bethke Elshtain is centrally concerned with combating what she sees as feminist attacks on the family. Ironically perhaps, the problems she identifies have arisen most directly in relation to abortion. The contemporary women's movement has tended to see a woman's right to abortion – her right to decide for herself whether or not to continue with a pregnancy – as the quintessentially feminist demand. A woman who cannot choose what is done with her body is no better than a slave; how could anyone else claim to make this decision? Yet almost as soon as it was articulated, 'a woman's right to choose' became a source of anxiety. It was such a defiant assertion of individual rights, such a refusal of social intervention. In most of the issues that have provoked feminist campaigns, the division between public and private was being identified as a crucial element in the subordination of women, something that excused society from its responsibilities for caring for the young and old, that confined women to a (lesser) realm they had not chosen to inhabit and, in such phrases as 'the Englishman's home is his castle', legitimated domestic violence. Over abortion, feminism seemed to be going the opposite way.

The slogan chanted on many demonstrations – 'not the church and not the state, women must decide their fate' – claimed absolute autonomy for women in choosing whether or not to bear a child and derived much of its power from the widely shared belief that having babies is a private affair. In the USA, the crucial case of Roe v. Wade was settled by reference to a woman's right of privacy, which in the words of the Supreme Court was 'broad enough to encompass a woman's decision whether or not to terminate her pregnancy' (cited in Petchesky 1986:290). As Rosalind Petchesky notes, this was not meant to vindicate a woman's right to choose, for the 1973 decision gave the doctor responsibility for making the choice and reserved to the state a right to intervene (to prohibit abortion) at later stages in the pregnancy. That said, the legal decision that did most to extend the availability of abortion to US women was based on a notion of the individual as autonomous in the private sphere. And in 1989, when this availability was being challenged in all quarters and state after state was introducing more restrictive legislation, the notion of abortion being a matter for the women themselves still retained amazing support. A national survey conducted by the *Los Angeles Times* revealed that, while 61 per cent of Americans thought abortion morally wrong and a stunning 57 per cent considered it murder, nonetheless 74 per cent of respondents believed abortion was a decision that must be made by each woman for herself (cited in Dworkin 1989).

Feminist have long been uneasy with the implications. Commenting on the breadth of support for a woman's right to decide for herself whether to have an abortion or not, Susan Himmelweit suggests that 'the popularity of the idea of private choice in reproduction is a reflection and acceptance of the existing division', in which having babies is a private, and of course female, concern (1980:67). People respond readily enough because it fits with their existing convictions – and yet these convictions themselves are part of what feminism has attacked. The case for greater social provision for children, for example, has often been argued on the grounds that children are *not* exclusively their mother's concern. With the exception of babies conceived by artificial insemination by donor, each child has both a father and a mother, so why is it only the latter who takes care of the child? Each child will grow up to contribute to the society, so why doesn't society do more to help? The modern counter-argument can all too easily be fuelled by the woman's right to choose whether or not to have babies: 'well, you chose to have them, so stop complaining and get on with the job.' It is hard (though not impossible) to argue both cases simultaneously, hard to call on fathers and/or society to shoulder more responsibility for those children who are born, and yet in the same breath deny the fathers or society any voice in making the decision.

For some socialist feminists, the argument then becomes contingent on the social arrangements for bringing up children. Thus as long as society makes the woman responsible for nurture and care and support, no one other than the woman can decide. But if and when societies do assume responsibility for the welfare of children, she can no longer claim this right. Once her 'private' choice has clearly 'public' effects – when, for example, her decision to have ten children instead of one means a substantial redirection of social resources – then we cannot say it is entirely her affair. It is worth noting (and is an indication of how strongly feminists have felt on the issue of abortion) that even here the examples given are usually of women who want more children not fewer. In this future scenario in which the care of children has become a social concern, the issue raised is not so much whether a woman can be forced to continue with a pregnancy that she does not want, but whether she can freely choose more children than the norm. Even among feminists who regard the right to choose as contingent on social conditions, the fact that it is women's bodies in which pregnancies occur remains a disturbing factor.

The issues of reproductive choice have generated much thoughtful literature (see, for example, Petchesky 1986 and Birke et al. 1990) and a lot of this revolves around the relationship between public and private and the extent to which any decision can be a matter for one individual alone. With further developments in reproductive technology, new dilemmas arise. Should, for example, a woman have the right to abort a foetus that happens to be of the wrong sex? Should a woman have the right to 'rent' out her womb as a surrogate mother? Are these also dimensions of 'a woman's right to choose'? There is no consensus on these questions, and within feminism there has been a strong anti-liberal tendency that has argued against certain kinds of choice (see Corea 1985).

Many maintain, however, that even in the best of all possible worlds, certain aspects of reproductive and sexual relations will remain irreducibly personal affairs. 'Can we really imagine', asks Rosalind Petchesky, 'the social conditions in which we would be ready to renounce control over our bodies and reproductive lives – to give over the decision as to whether, when and with whom we will bear children to the "community as a whole"?' (1986:13). If women are not free to make such choices for themselves, then they are being compelled into pregnancy and childbirth and this 'is incompatible with the existence of women as moral agents and social beings' (p. 388). To link this with the arguments developed by Carole Pateman, a womb is not something that can be rented out like a house, or taken under legal charge by a judge who decides a foetus must live. The body is part of the self, and it is only the extraordinary male conceptions of the individual that could ever have conceived of them as so separate and distinct.

If abortion is the testing ground for dissolving all differences between public and private, then most feminists fail. When it comes down to it, they do want to retain distinctions between some areas or activities that are open to public decision and others that should remain personal concerns. The argument does not usually depend on how democratically public decisions are made, for women will want to retain control over certain aspects of their lives no matter how impressive the procedures have become. At the same time, however, feminists have wanted to challenge the enforced separation between public and private, and though this may sound too much like having one's cake and eating it, it is not, in fact, inconsistent. As Iris Young has argued (1987), there ought to be certain aspects of our lives from which we are entitled to exclude others, about which we can say they are nobody's affair but our own. (We will argue endlessly about what fits into this category, but that is not to say the category itself is absurd.) Equally important, however, is that there should be no aspect of our lives which we are compelled to keep private. There is no inconsistency, for example, in saying that our sexuality should be our private concern but that homophobia should be on the public agenda. In similar vein, there is no inconsistency in saying that abortion is a decision we must make for ourselves, but that the treatment of children should be a public concern.

Most feminist writing implies a distinction of sorts between public and private – and the fact that Kate Millett is so often invoked as the example of what not to do suggests that there are not too many to choose from who have abandoned all distinction! In terms of democracy, this means that the sphere of sexual and family relations cannot be treated in exactly the same way as the sphere of work or the sphere of conventional politics. First, there are some decisions that must be regarded as an individual and not a social affair, and under any conditions that I can envisage, a woman's right to decide for herself whether or not to continue with a pregnancy remains the clearest example of this. When women are denied access to abortion, they are being denied the freedom to make this choice themselves, and are being treated as if their bodies belonged to somebody else. Democracy is not supposed to coexist with slavery, and no society can present itself as fully democratic if it compels women into unwanted pregnancy and childbirth. This seems to me indisputable, but it is worth noting that this version of democracy has a markedly liberal tone.

In the more mundane (if often more pressing) areas of who cleans the house and who cooks the meals, the women's movement has certainly said that democracy should be extended to the private sphere. People rarely make any formal analogy between the equal right to vote in elections and an equal say in household affairs: it is hardly a question of secret ballots on who cleans the bathroom, or formal majorities on what to have for tea. But when women have noted that men presume the authority to take major decisions because they bring in the money on which the household survives, there are strong resonances of what is a classic argument for democracy. Income and wealth should be entirely irrelevant; each individual should have an equal voice. (Women also, of course, argue that incomes should be equalized, and query the complacent formalism of liberal ideas. But the claim on equal standing in household decisions is not made to depend on this.)

Anything that is a decision should be taken by equals. Things that have been taken for granted as if they were ordained by nature should be decided by open discussion and mutual consent. It should not be assumed, for example, that there is a particular division of labour between the sexes: that the woman cleans the house and the man cleans the car; that the woman gives up her job when a baby is born; that the man's occupation is always more important; that the whole family moves when he gets a new job. All these should enter the realm of democratic discussion, to be treated as matters of choice. It is part of the success of the women's movement – and simultaneously of the strength of what the movement must contest – that household inequalities do not depend only on men asserting their authority, but as often as not on men and women sharing an uncritical consensus about how things should be. Even so, interviews with women workers continue to throw up the comment that 'my husband wouldn't let me work while the baby was young' or 'my husband would never allow me to work nights'. Important decisions are still taken by men.

On abortion, women have demanded the right to take a decision by themselves and not be dictated to by what others say or do. But in other aspects, too, there is a limit to how much we can assimilate private and public spheres. 'Household' democracy, in particular, is not really a matter of regulation, imposition, guarantee. There are all kinds of social intervention that can help make relations between the sexes more democratic, and various ways in which public policy or public resources can contribute to a process of change. The provision of refuges and affordable accommodation can give more women a choice about leaving relationships that are beyond redemption; changes in the hours that men and women work can increase the chances for equalizing the distribution of household tasks; changes in the practices of mortgage companies, landlords and insurance offices can give women more of a say. All these can empower women, making it more possible for them to claim their place as equals and encouraging the practices of democracy in the home. None of these, however, can dictate what goes on between lovers or husbands and wives – and with the exception of bodily injury, most people prefer it this way. At the end of the day, what happens will depend on the individuals themselves, on how much they insist on change.

Means and ends This is no news to the women's movement, and indeed it is much of what 'the personal is political' has meant to feminists over the last twenty years. Part of the slipperiness of the slogan is that it takes us out of our personal preoccupations and experiences, and simultaneously lets us treat these experiences as the political centre of our life. Thus, on the one hand, it has helped women see that what they thought of as peculiar to themselves (personal, unique and perhaps basically their fault) may be part of a general pattern of sexual relations that is then available to political change. On the other hand, it gives women the confidence to claim the kind of changes they can already make (refusing to cook the dinner or type the leaflet, maybe even throwing him out) as politically important. Politics then becomes something other than procedures or rules or programmes for change. It is what we do in our everyday life.

Politics had become associated with alien or grandiose concerns, either because it was thought to happen in particular places (from which women were absent), or because it dealt with matters of earth-shattering importance (on which women could have nothing to say). Contemporary feminism has challenged this, theoretically in terms of the abstract way men have thought about power, and practically in saying politics has no integrity until it is grounded in everyday life. Drawing attention to the detailed texture of our daily lives, 'the personal is political' has claimed a continuum between those things that were previously considered the most trivial and minor and those to which the term politics could be confidently attached. But instead of referring to a particular place (the household), this version of 'the personal' stresses aspects that will be present in every activity, no matter where or when it takes place. This is perhaps the most characteristic of all the meanings associated with the slogan and the one that will be most familiar to those who have been active in the women's movement over the last decades. What implications does it have for democracy?

When women in the civil rights or socialist movement said the personal was political, part of what they were stressing was the relationship between means and end. There was something pretty suspect about organizations that could see themselves as dedicated to liberation but treated the women involved as if they had no abilities or minds of their own. The ideals were being subverted by the daily practice, and yet most men seemed to think this a silly complaint. The new women's movement was convinced that it did indeed matter and consistently emphasized the ways women related to one another as a crucial part of what the movement was about. You could not claim to be involved in a politics of liberation if you unthinkingly exploited other people's time and energies and continually put people down. The division of labour mattered, so did inequalities in confidence or capacities, and so did any separation into leaders and led. Feminism meant thinking about all these issues, regarding the way you organized as something that was as important and revealing as your goals.

The attempt to sustain a non-hierarchical movement proved highly problematic, and in the next chapter I will look in more detail at the women's movement experience of participatory democracy and the kinds of difficulties and lessons this threw up. Here I want to explore the more general implications of the argument, which in Britain at least has contributed to a major review of what political activity is about. The women's movement drew on its concern with forms of organization and inter-personal relations to develop a radically participatory notion of democracy, and this was applied not only to women's groups but to every aspect of political life. To take one prominent example, when feminists campaigned for more nursery provision, they devoted considerable energy to considering the ways in which nurseries should be organized, the representational structures that would give voice to both workers and parents, the kind of non-sexist activities that should be developed for the children, whether and how men should be involved. It was never just a matter of where the money would come from, and because of anxieties about bureaucratic regulation, the women's movement has often been in two minds about whether nurseries should be set up by the state (see, for instance, Rowbotham 1989: ch. 8). The quantity of child provision was only half the question. Equally important was whether the nursery could be organized in a democratic and enabling way.

These concerns ran through virtually every activity of the last twenty years, from nurseries to refuges to bookshops to caucuses in unions. The emphasis on means as well as ends was not exclusive to feminism, for it also reflected the wider radicalism of the day. But the women's movement can legitimately claim to be its foremost practitioner and has thereby contributed to a growing awareness of how much these 'details' matter. In the case of Britain, this was to be amply demonstrated in the course of the 1980s by the influence of *Beyond The Fragments* (Rowbotham et al. 1979) which drew on the experience of the women's movement to challenge the authoritarianism of socialist groups. The initiative momentarily spawned a near-movement, with conferences and day schools and newsletters. And even when this impetus died away, the notion of 'pre-figurative forms' remained in much of the British debate.

Socialist discussion drew (often explicitly) on women's movement arguments about the relationship between means and ends. The way we do things was increasingly recognized as being as important as what we set out to do, for we can pre-figure the future society in the relations we establish among ourselves. We send out messages by the kind of organizational structures we create, but also by the way we talk, write and play. The issue goes further than the classic question raised by critics of Leninism, for it is not just a matter of there being a dissonance between two things that are clearly 'political', like the aims and the structure of the organization. The women's movement suggested that there can be contradictions between what anyone would consider part of politics and things as seemingly irrelevant as what we wear or what jokes make us laugh.

The idea that people should be consistent is not peculiar to feminism, and the other side of the coin is the infamous moralism that political movements so often produce. There is a thin line between what is positive in saying that people should practise what they preach and what is negative in arraigning them when they fail to live up to their ideals. As the next chapter will indicate, feminism has often fallen victim to the more destructive side but it should be said in its favour that at least in principle this was the opposite of the intent. The women's movement has made more than most of the connection between personal experience and political ideal, and in a way that scrutinized especially the ideals. The practice of consciousness-raising groups clearly expressed this. Political aims and objectives should be grounded in personal experience and, instead of occupying a distinctively 'political' terrain, should arise out of and speak back to each individual's life.

This warns against the kind of altruism or arrogance that wants to revolutionize the lives of those further afield yet remains blindly complacent over conditions closer to home. Perhaps even more significantly, it warns against the presumption that we know what matters in advance. For many of the women who formed the nucleus of the contemporary movement, politics had previously operated as a kind of thought-police, dictating which things were relevant and which beside the point. Feminism tried to break this pattern, creating a context in which women could talk through and discuss issues without any preconceived limits. What was or was not political would emerge through these discussions. Nothing would emerge if the restrictions were set in advance.

The stretching of definitions is one of the best things that feminism has done for democracy. But it is also in some ways the least controversial. Rows will continue to rage in political parties or trade unions or work-based committees over what counts as politically significant; what issues should be discussed and whether the way we discuss them matters as much as what we say. Yet the basic idea that politics means different things to different people is not fundamentally contentious, and I think most people will accept that the boundaries around politics can change. As long as feminists confine themselves to changing and enlarging the public agenda – as Iris Young puts it, making public issues out of practices claimed too trivial for public discussion – then 'the personal is political' can be accommodated within existing democratic discourse. I do not say this to disparage its significance or to underestimate the forces that range themselves against novel definitions. But as long as feminists accept that there *is* a public agenda, that there is a distinction that matters between public and private spheres, then the argument is not fundamentally disruptive. It is when the distinction between public and private space is queried that things begin to get sticky.

The public arena Let me return to the arguments associated with civic republicanism in order to make this more clear. When Hannah Arendt defines politics in terms of the pursuit of public happiness or the taste for public freedom, she is employing a terminology almost the opposite to that adopted within the contemporary women's movement, though anyone who has experienced the heady delights of political involvement will have some inkling of what she means. The impulse that drives people into an endless round of meetings, demonstrations and discussion groups must be more than the imperative of material need, and leaving aside those cases where politics has become a career, it fits in some way with a taste for 'public freedom'. When people complain that they cannot arouse others from their private affairs – when, for example, an exhaustive leafleting of twenty streets has produced only one new face at the meeting – their despair echoes Arendt's ideals. Few of us may live up to her other definition of politics as the striving for excellence 'regardless not only of social status and administrative office but even of achievement and congratulation' (1963:280), but again we probably know what she means. Certainly the women's movement was quick to spot the distracting appeals of the 'star system' and to query the good faith of those whose political involvement seemed a route to public acclaim.

Yet in most ways the principles of republican democracy seem antagonistic to women's movement concerns. None of its theorists is an enthusiast for dissolving the boundaries between public and private, or for transforming the way decisions are made in every arena of social life. Those who have devoted their energies to democratizing the 'little world' of factory or office or community are at best patronized for their limited ambitions, and at worst criticized for a dangerous distraction. There seems no obvious bridge between this and feminist perspectives. When women argue that 'democratic ideals and politics have to be put into practice in the kitchen, the nursery and the bedroom' (Pateman 1983:216) they are pointing in just the opposite direction.

Feminists have criticized the orthodox division between public and private, presenting a powerful and radical challenge to existing notions of democracy. They have broadened our under-

standing of the preconditions for democratic equality, and
brought into the discussion the sexual division of labour at home
and at work. They have challenged (though with some important
reservations) the notion that what goes on in private is a private
concern, and made what seems an unanswerable case for democratizing relations and decisions in the home. They have enlarged
our conception of the practices that are relevant, pulling into the
orbit of democracy the way we talk to one another, the way we
organize, the way we write. They have attached themselves to a
vision of democracy as something that matters in every detail and
wherever we are. With all these wonderful extensions, do feminists remain stuck in what Sheldon Wolin (1982:28) considers the
politics of their own backyard?

The question is posed most starkly by those who accuse feminists of collapsing into the cosiness of inter-personal dynamics, and
who cite as examples the counter-cultural focus on lifestyle politics, or the more recent growth of feminist therapies. In either
case, the equation of the personal with the political is said to have
legitimated women in retreating from political concerns. In the
first instance, women abandoned their efforts at changing the
world and chose to live out an exclusive alternative with those of
like mind. The rhetoric might sound defiant and, if we take Mary
Daly as a possible exemplar, claimed a more risky and less com-
promised existence than that available to those who continued to
engage with the masculine world. But it hardly mattered whether
the choice was expressed in the cloying language of wonderful
women or the angry denunciation of patriarchy and men.
Whichever it was, women had stepped out of the political arena to
build their strength in an alternative world. In the case of feminist
therapies, women were said to be turning even further in on
themselves. Here there was not even the pretence of constructing
a different kind of world: just an unhealthy obsession with the
problems of self.

These aspects of contemporary feminism have very little to do
with democracy, beyond perhaps a shared language of partnership or discussion. But they are also so far from exhausting what
the women's movement is about that I do not find this particularly
disturbing. The more troublesome issues arise where the women's
movement has clearly engaged with democratic concerns. Where
there is an explicit focus on democracy, feminism has tended to
associate itself with those who argue for a revitalized and reconsti-
tuted civil society. Few have noticed, fewer still commented on,

the division that is growing up between those who emphasize civil society as the focus for democratic development and those who stress the state or, more broadly, the public sphere (for one exception, see Pierson 1989). For those in the first camp, the main focus will be on the layer of social activity that is intermediate between the personal, or individual, and the state. They will aim to multiply therefore the contexts in which people can choose to assert control over their lives, contexts which include our places of work but also community-based centres and voluntary organizations. As John Keane puts it, in a list that makes direct overtures to feminism: 'the self-governed enterprise, the democratic trade union, the rape crisis centre, the gay and lesbian collective, the housing co-operative, and other public spheres of civil society' (1988a:145). This seems very close to what feminists have been saying and doing over the last twenty years. It extends the principles of participation out of their previous workplace confines and projects a notion of democracy as something that should permeate every social activity and sphere. But, implicitly or explicitly, it suggests that democracy is a matter of building blocks: the more we have the better the edifice will be. In this sense, it dodges the relationship between particular and general and denies any peculiarity about a public sphere.

Writers like Arendt or Wolin would, by contrast, claim a qualitative leap from the specific to the general and would say that however democratic we are in running our rape crisis centre, we are not yet engaged in politics *per se*. Politics arises only when we are faced with people who are different and have to work out with them our common and shared concerns. Or, as Benjamin Barber puts it, 'essential contestability is the premise of politics' (1984: 157), and politics only happens when we do not agree. This criterion alone will not dismiss the rape crisis centre from the realm of politics, for disagreement may be furious and any decisions strongly contested. But think of the next stage up. Members from the centre attend a meeting of the elected council which controls local finances, in order to put their case for funding. Here they represent just one among many demands on resources and can only put their case as effectively and clearly as possible, making sure all councillors know what the issues are. Obviously they would hope that some of the councillors would volunteer to further their cause, but if all the elected members went in with their votes fixed (each one nobbled beforehand by some group), the meeting would be a depressing occasion. Discussion would be desultory and irrelevant, and each vote would have been decided in advance. The groups with no automatic allies in the council (this would very likely include the crisis centre) would complain bitterly, for they would have been deprived of their chance to influence the meeting and win new support to their side. And on any definition of democracy, their complaints would surely be justified. We do not want politics reduced to a mere counting of numbers, with all decisions sewn up in advance. Imagine that someone from the centre was also an elected member of the council: most people would hope she could stand back a bit from the centre's interests and not just campaign on a single concern. We would expect her decisions on the council to be influenced by the knowledge and experience she brought from the rape crisis centre, but we would not want her to be a cipher for a single group and unable to connect with other concerns.

As in the preceding discussion of the representation of women, it is important to separate out two aspects. The first is the desirability of ensuring that our representatives include people from previously marginalized groups: there are all too many councils on which no one person understands what a rape crisis centre involves. But the second is that there are levels of representation, and that failing to acknowledge these would collapse all levels of decision-making into one. There is a connection, and some continuity, between the specific and the general, but there is also an important and distinctive shift. When the small collective that produces a feminist newsletter struggles to work in democratic fashion, its members are learning the kind of confidence, competence and respect for the opinions of others that will help them change for the better any other organization to which they subsequently belong. In this sense, every democratized forum in civil society is a kind of building block out of which we get democracy as a whole; and the more there are, the better things will be. But there are also things that the members of the collective will have to *un*learn in a different situation. Small collectives often generate an all-enveloping enthusiasm, in which nothing else seems of comparable importance or worth. This is not a helpful attitude to carry into a wider arena, for it can prematurely close debate or understanding. We cannot, and should not, be expected to 'leave ourselves behind' when we enter the political arena, but we ought nonetheless to be able to look at ourselves in a different kind of light. In this sense, extending democracy is not just about democratizing all our practices in every aspect of our lives. There remains a distinction between the general and the particular, and it is important not to blur this divide.

For a variety of reasons, then, I am arguing that we *do* need a distinction between private and public, and that rather than abandoning this distinction, the emphasis should be on uncoupling it from the division between women and men. First, there are some decisions which will remain individual ones, and no matter how thoroughly democratized public debate and decision-making may become, there are matters we will want to reserve to ourselves. The clearest example of this is a woman's decision about continuing or terminating a pregnancy, but a less gender-specific example might be the choices we make about our sexuality. Second, even within the much larger category of decisions where a number of people are involved and each is then entitled to an equal voice, there is a distinction between spheres within which democracy can be imposed and spheres within which it should be enabled. If we take the simplest definition of democracy as saying that everyone should have a vote and nobody more than one, there will be certain areas where this can and should be enforced by law (it should be illegal to vote twice in elections) and others where it would be nonsense to have formal regulation. Feminism has brought the domestic sphere much more clearly into the orbit of democratic debate, but the argument is that women should be empowered so that they can insist on the equality themselves, and in this sense it still retains a distinction.

Finally, the equation of the personal with the political has drawn attention to the details of how people relate and organize and has thus been linked to the democratization of whatever association (including places of work) we find ourselves in. On this point, however, feminists have sometimes acted as if there were an amorphous continuum in which there are no distinctions beyond those of size. Here, too, we need to differentiate. There is a difference between extending control over decisions to everyone involved in a particular venture or place of work, and increasing participation in what has been traditionally defined as politics. The one does not lead inexorably to the other. Feminism rightly queries the exclusive emphasis on 'politics' as conventionally defined and has stressed the often more immediate issues of taking control where we work and live. This positive insistence on the democratization of everyday life should not become a substitute for a more lively and vital political life.

5

PARADOXES OF PARTICIPATION

The women's movement is now commonly divided into two waves, the first sweeping over Europe and America in the mid-nineteenth century, the second crashing against the post-war consensus just over a hundred years later. Questions of internal democracy have been important to both phases. For many of those active in the first wave, for example, it was the experience of working in organizations or campaigns which nonetheless denied women a voice that precipitated them from feminist thinking to feminist action. The origins of the suffrage movement in the USA is an obvious case in point. Women had been actively engaged in anti-slavery work – raising funds, collecting signatures on petitions, speaking on public platforms – for a number of years, but the controversy over what role was appropriate to their sex split the US anti-slavery movement. One faction would only accept women in auxiliary societies, while the other conceded the full right to join. This more radical wing then included four women in its delegation to the 1840 World Anti-slavery Convention; the conference refused to let them in. Historians frequently cite this experience, along with the friendships and alliances that developed in its wake, as directly responsible for the 1848 Seneca Falls Convention, which is usually seen as the moment when the US women's movement began (Banks 1981:21–3).

Who participated in decisions and how decisions were to be made were questions that remained significant. But the concern with internal democracy coexisted with its opposite, for as a movement that had to challenge the most strongly held beliefs on the position of women, feminism relied on women of unusual charisma and courage. Tremendous importance attached to the activities and leadership of key individuals; women like Josephine Butler and Christabel Pankhurst were almost worshiped by those they inspired. In the case of Christabel Pankhurst at least, this came to conflict with the broader democratic ideals. As the battle for women's suffrage reached its height in Britain, the Women's Social and Political Union was restructured along selfconsciously military lines, with Christabel Pankhurst the exiled general who directed the campaign from abroad. A series of organizational splits weakened and reduced the WSPU, and the over-centralized command structure was invariably cited as part of what precipitated each break. Democracy or its absence was a big issue in the suffrage campaign.

The contemporary women's movement emerged in the 1960s in the context of a generalized radicalism in the liberal democracies, in which ' "participatory democracies" ... appeared everywhere like fragile bubbles' (Mansbridge 1980:22). In one neighbourhood after another, in one country after another, small groups of people with little money but plenty of energy decided to act: to organize a free school independent of the state; to produce and distribute an irreverent alternative to the local newspaper; to take over empty buildings and turn them to community use. In virtually every case, the principles of self-organization were conceived as intrinsic to the political goals, and most of these groups attempted (if with varying degrees of success) to divide up their work and make their decisions in an appropriately democratic way. Worker co-operatives used the weekly assembly as their alternative to management's boardroom decisions, and they often equalized wages to eliminate distinctions in status and power. Community groups tried to rotate responsibilities among all members. Meetings frequently commenced with a discussion of how to hold a discussion, and once unquestioned procedures – such as having a chairman, motions, amendments, and then finally majority votes – became themselves a topic of debate.

For the women's movement, questions of internal democracy returned to the centre of the stage, this time imbued with an almost anarchist critique of authority, an intensely egalitarian approach. In most of the newly formed women's groups, any kind of hierarchy was automatically suspect. Meetings were informal and only loosely structured; in a comparison that was to be frequently invoked in the early years, they were patterned on a gathering of friends. Women came together to share their experiences – the consciousness-raising that was such an important part of early involvement – and to work out actions and campaigns. In these meetings no one voice should ever claim to be more definitive than another. By the same token, no one woman should be able to assume responsibility for the more interesting or influential tasks. Expertise and authority should be divided and shared: democracy was conceived not as a matter of representation or accountability but as a genuine equalization of power.

In her introduction to the first anthology of writings from the US women's liberation movement, Robin Morgan illustrates some of this early vision with her account of the lot system and the disc system, both devised by women's groups in the United States. The first was a way of pre-empting the inequalities that come from the division of labour. All the tasks associated with the group were divided up according to whether they were creative or routine, and each member then drew lots for one of each kind. The second system tackled the inequalities that arise in group discussion. Every woman began the meeting with an identical number of discs. Each time she spoke she 'spent' one of these, and once she had run through her entire supply she was expected to keep herself quiet.

> The first time this system was tried, the apocryphal story goes, no one in the room had any discs left after fifteen minutes. The second meeting was slow almost to silence because everyone was hoarding her discs. Gradually, the device worked its way into everyone's consciousness as a symbol for the need to listen to each other, and not interrupt or monopolize the conversation. (Morgan 1970:xxviii)

Overly mechanistic as these examples now sound, the ideals they reflect were widely shared. That each woman should be equally respected was almost a founding principle, and equal respect is hard to sustain where there are clearly leaders and led.

Most of the radicals of the period had an idea of sharing things around – tasks, expertise, influence, the length of time each member could speak – but this radical equality of participation assumed a particular significance for women. Every organization has its division of labour between 'mental' and 'manual', creative and routine tasks, but the long association of women with office work has usually guaranteed that they are the ones who type the leaflets, take the minutes and bring the tea. Every organization has its complement of good talkers and silent listeners, but the construction of male and female identities has usually meant that women are disproportionately represented in the listening camp. What could appear as a general problem to other radical movements became for women a matter of the power between women and men. The women's movement was thus acutely sensitive to the relations of dominance and subordination that emerge in the course of discussions or get reflected in the distribution of work. An unequal distribution of skills was thought to be inevitably correlated with an unequal distribution of power.

Especially in the first years of the movement, there was, then, an emphasis on either sharing or rotating responsibilities. The first national newsletter in the USA – *Voice of the Women's Liberation Movement* – was edited by different women for each issue; the national newsletter of the UK movement – *WIRES* – was produced by different groups that volunteered for the job. Papers that circulated at conferences were commonly written by groups rather than individuals. The conferences themselves would be organized not by an elected co-ordinating committee, but simply by collectives that had proposed themselves for the task. The occasional disarray that went along with this was thought well worth it, for a range of skills and responsibilities was in principle being made accessible to every woman, and no one could use her superior knowledge to claim for herself superior power.

In the 1970s at least, this anti-authoritarianism infected even the more 'professional' women's organizations. In *The Politics of Women's Liberation*, Jo Freeman reports that by 1973–4 the 'younger wing' of the US movement had successfully carried its ideals of participatory democracy into the more orthodox arrangements of the National Organization of Women (NOW), and that the organization was under increasing pressure to change its overly hierarchical practices (1975:ch. 3). The texture of their meetings then became an important political issue. As in the smaller, more overtly radical, groups, there was a stress on informality, on blending the logic of argument with the passion of personal experience and on avoiding a confrontational or domineering style. Unlike the 'younger wing', NOW continued to proceed by way of motions, debates and majority votes. But Freeman notes that it had begun to reject 'the assumption that "one side must win" for the assumption that, with sufficient effort invested, a compromise acceptable to all can be found' (p. 94).

Whether it was the older or younger wing, there had to be a way of taking decisions. Women's groups had to work out their plan of action in any campaigns, while national conferences had to formulate priorities and demands. In the case of Britain, for example, the initial demands were extended and revised in plenary sessions at later annual conferences; the very sharp disagreements over wording and emphasis that surfaced in the 1978 meeting heralded the end of the national conference. Decisions were made, and the outcome was felt to matter, and yet the conference was not conceived as a representative institution. Like the citizens' assemblies of ancient Greece, the national conferences were open to all: all that is, except men, and with a frequent question mark over women journalists who were reporting for the national press. The size of each conference depended only on how many women chose to attend, and while the choice about where the next conference should be held was frequently debated in terms of equalizing access from all over the country, there was no formal mechanism for ensuring regional balance. Each woman spoke for herself, not as a delegate from an affiliated group, and where there was a vote each woman counted just as one.

In many political organizations – trade union, political party, pressure group – meetings and conferences are primarily about making decisions. In the women's liberation movement, this was a subsidiary feature, and the emphasis was much more on meeting, talking, acting, sharing experiences and ideas. Politics and friendship were often elided, perhaps most strikingly in this quote from Robin Morgan:

> This is not a movement one 'joins'. There are no rigid structures or membership cards. The Women's Liberation Movement exists where three or four friends or neighbours decide to meet regularly over coffee and talk about their personal lives. It also exists in the cells of women's jails, in the welfare lines, in the supermarket, the factory, the convent, the farm, the maternity ward, the streetcorner, the old ladies' home, the kitchen, the steno pool, the bed. It exists in your mind, and in the political and personal insights that you can contribute to change and shape and help its growth. (1970:xxxvi)

In similar vein, though without so completely dissolving the distinction between political action and meeting your friends, one London group noted in 1971 the benefits they derived from organizing on a small, local basis. They were always bumping into one another outside as well as inside meetings, thus 'cutting down the schizophrenia of most political action' (in Wandor 1971: 105–6). Instead of seeing politics as something 'out there' or regarding meetings as a duty and a task, women could experience their involvement as an extension of their everyday life.

Jane Mansbridge has noted that the early Greeks also made an explicit connection between democracy and friendship, and in *Beyond Adversary Democracy* she quotes Aristotle as saying that 'friendship appears to hold city-states together' (1980:9). Where this connection is more than rhetorical, she argues, it will increase the desire to be active, for once the boundary between politics and friendship is breached, then 'the costs of participation, of which some make so much, do not feel heavy. Citizens "fly to the assemblies" as if to meet their friends. They value the time they spend on common affairs' (p. 9). The association between politics and friendship, and the way this can increase the excitement and interest in meetings, was certainly a feature of the women's liberation movement – though perhaps particularly so for those who had no children, or who had not yet exhausted themselves in years of political life. For many women, the movement became their life, the women's group their closest friends. In such a context, the extra time it takes to do things collectively rather than on your own is not necessarily seen as a cost, and while it can be unbearable to attend yet another over-long meeting with people you dislike, the experience is very different when the others at the meeting are friends.

It was not long, of course, before people noted the limits of friendship (the phrase comes from Mansbridge 1976), the two most serious being that it is impossible to include everyone in the circle of your friends, and that it is hard to disagree without more fundamentally falling out. Despite the rapid growth of the women's movement, with new groups springing up all over the place and ideas spreading fast from one country to another, it was apparent to most of those involved that they were a pretty unrepresentative bunch. Mostly in their twenties or thirties; overwhelmingly white; very often college-educated and holding a degree. There seemed to be a trade-off between the intensity with which those who *were* involved committed themselves, and the capacity of the movement to extend its appeal. This in turn seemed to be related to precisely those aspects that had brought politics and friendship together. For those already involved, the absence of formal structures, the informality, the shared jokes and references, were a part of what the movement was about. These very same phenomena could seem mysterious and exclusionary to those not yet accepted as friends.

This makes a neat entry point for the unsympathetic critic, who can draw on the usual range of complaints against participatory democracy to note that this is unequal and unfair. Had Giovanni Sartori, for example, deigned to notice the women's movement, he would have had a wonderful time. Here we have precisely that equation of more democracy with more participation – and precisely the anticipated problems, that only a few women will attend. Membership becomes self-selecting and exclusive, while the time constraints that Michael Walzer noted work even more acutely where women are involved. How many can reorganize their lives to include the evening meetings, daytime actions, weekend conferences that the women's movement usually entailed? Yet activity and involvement were being presented as the only way to belong, leaving no room for the 'half-virtuous' woman who had neither time nor inclination for this.

It is a considerable tribute to contemporary feminism that these problems were all aired internally, and attention extended to include many more. The recent experience of the women's liberation movement thus provides us with one of the fullest explorations of the strengths and weaknesses of participatory democracy, and though the issues that arose have precursors in theoretical literature, they are in this context more nuanced and detailed. The movement that is sometimes hailed from outside as a model of participatory democracy is also one of the richer sources for thinking about participation and its problems. Among the problems that feminists began to raise, five stand out as particularly pertinent:

1   By refusing to distinguish political from other aspects of equality and insisting on a thoroughgoing equalization of involvement and skills, the movement was forcing many women to deny their talents and abilities and was wasting their energy and time. Democracy was becoming inefficient.

2   By relying so heavily on face-to-face meetings, women's groups were sending conflict underground and producing what was a false consensus. Women were being pressured to pretend to agree.

3   By refusing to formalize the structures of decision-making, women's groups and conferences were also refusing to develop

procedures for accountability. No leaders or elites were acknowledged, but this meant that *de facto* leaders and elites went
unchecked.

4 By the same token, the absence of formal procedures for membership, delegation or representation meant that the movement
could never say for whom or for how many it spoke. It could not
then engage with authority in influencing politics outside; it could
not claim the legitimacy of a representative body.

5 By making the meeting such a central part of involvement, the
movement inevitably limited its membership, ending up as an
unrepresentative few.

These issues were raised and discussed from early in the history of
the women's liberation movement, so early indeed that they
predate the moment at which most women would say that they
'joined'. A number of them surface, for example, in Jo Freeman's
The Tyranny of Structurelessness, a highly influential essay which
circulated inside the US movement in 1970, was reprinted that
same year in the *Berkeley Journal of Sociology* and was subsequently
copied and distributed in a variety of pamphlet forms. The problems of participation were voiced almost in unison with the ideals;
in exploring these five topics, I shall be drawing on what was
almost continuous discussion, anxiety and debate.

A democratic division of labour It is innocuous enough to say
that democracy implies equal respect and most people would see
the two as connected – at the very least as not opposed. The
difficulty comes when we think about what makes equal respect
more than a pleasant injunction. In particular, how does the
notion of equal respect survive that plethora of educational, class,
or just natural differences of which we are usually acutely aware?
It is part of the strength of minimalist democracy that the question
does not necessarily arise, for the precise quality of respect you
feel for the person who occupies the polling booth next to you is
barely significant – and should not affect his or her right to vote. In
the face-to-face context of a meeting, however, differences can
dominate the scene, and the liberal case against participatory
democracy has substantially rested on this. Decision-making
based on meetings is almost invariably weighted towards those
with the confidence to articulate their position. Since these are

usually the ones already favoured with wealth, education and power, the meeting may then be less democratic than the ballot, where each counts only as one.

The women's movement's preoccupation with equalizing skills and contributions can be read as an answer to this charge. The shift from passive to active democracy will only work when it combines with some beginning of an answer to this problem; failing this, it may indeed make matters worse. Equal respect has to be made something more than a form of words. Given the power that attaches to superior skill, that means changing the way tasks are distributed and the context in which ideas are discussed. In the short-term, people will have to unlearn the assumption that those who speak with confidence and clarity are therefore more worthy of our ears; in the longer term, they will need to recognize that what have been considered 'natural' talents and skills can, on the contrary, be taught and passed on. Rotating responsibilities – for producing the next leaflet, for introducing the next discussion, for writing up the group's report – can play a crucial part here. The sharing of skills makes it possible for people to learn to do things they previously thought beyond them. It helps demystify particular jobs that previously carried too much influence and power. It prevents those with highly valued skills from escaping their share of mundane work. It makes equal respect a substantial affair.

The general direction of this argument still strikes me as correct. The problem is how far it should go. Within the women's movement there was greater educational homogeneity than in the population as a whole. In addition, the majority of women were novices to the tasks they took on, and there was more an atmosphere of everyone having to learn. Despite these favourable conditions, it proved impossible to apply the principles of a democratic division of labour in a consistent and thoroughgoing way. Where it was clear that some women were better at certain jobs than others, it seemed absurd not to make use of their skills, and though the ideal was that others would then be learning the jobs, not all women proved to be good teachers.

The most serious difficulty, however, is not the potential 'waste' of energy and time. Jane Mansbridge (1980) notes in her study of a 1970s crisis centre that the extra time devoted to consensus decision-making (each worker spent as much as seven hours on meetings each week) contributed to a level of mutual trust and understanding that was almost indispensable to the work of the centre. In similar fashion, the extra time it took women's groups to write a leaflet or reach a consensus on what action to pursue cannot be regarded as pure waste. The efforts made to work collectively promoted a kind of commitment that is rarely, if ever, inspired by those tightly-run meetings that are brilliantly chaired and always end exactly on time. The efforts also had their practical effect: women really did learn new skills.

With all its seeming amateurism, the women's movement has had an extraordinary impact on the way in which women are now perceived, and events have not confirmed Jo Freeman's somewhat rash prediction that the small group structure, with its overly egalitarian (non)division of labour, would make the movement 'politically inefficacious' (1984:13). But in its more extreme versions, the principle of a fully democratic division of labour *is* utopian, and where it nonetheless remains as a desirable and achievable goal, it can become a damaging source of tension. No group will be able to unravel at will what has been wrapped around us from our earliest days; and even if it can be shown that difference is social not natural, no group can hope to eliminate all distinction. The difference, for example, between those who listen and those who talk can be very substantially modified – and some individuals can seem totally transformed – but even after years in the most sympathetic of environments, a distinction usually remains. This is not of itself a problem, for though the notion of equal respect should impel us to re-examine our assumptions and practices, it does not depend on us all becoming the same. But when total equalization becomes the aim, everything is bound to fall short. When this is additionally conceived as each individual's responsibility, it slips over too easily into being each individual's fault.

Many women have described how they felt pressured into a pretence that they knew nothing; others how they felt patronized by the silence of those who were keeping themselves quiet. The ideal had been set too high, which meant that women were often more disturbed by what was objectively less of a problem. Approximating closer than most organizations to their egalitarian, democratic ideals, women's groups were nonetheless more severe in their complaints; and individuals who on any conventional scale were remarkably free from authoritarian presumptions often found themselves under attack. I have no evidence beyond impressions, but I suspect that this helped to generate considerable scepticism towards egalitarian ideals of democracy and that, despairing of what seemed utopian standards, too many feminists lost confidence in much more moderate ideals. The women's movement rightly linked democratic equality to a more substantial equality in contributions and skills, but as happens so often in the history of democracy, the very real insight will be weakened when the connection is made too tight.

Philip Green (1985a) argues that democratic politics rests on a substantial social equality, and that it will remain incoherent as long as people are 'fixed' by their class, race, gender, education, income. Job rotation across different skills and throughout people's lives is then a condition for citizen equality. This seems to me correct, as does the further step the women's movement took in arguing for substantial equality within political movements, and challenging inequalities in the group's division of labour. The supposed inefficiency that results from this is overstated. The more serious problem is that when the standard is set at too elevated a level, everyone is guaranteed to fail. We need here a bit of the 'value management' Giovanni Sartori calls for in his *Theory of Democracy Revisited* (1987): not, as he proposes, by dropping all reference to a participatory model, but more modestly by acknowledging limits to what the most democratic of organizations can do.

Face-to-face meetings: conflict sent underground In her analysis of two examples of participatory democracy – the crisis centre with its seven hours of meetings and the annual town meetings of a small Vermont town – Jane Mansbridge identifies two related phenomena. In both of the case studies, there was a significant overlap between politics and friendship, and in the context of a face-to-face meeting this meant people could be intimidated from expressing their opinions, for they did not want to offend and they feared to disagree. The other side of the coin was that they made themselves more angry and antagonistic than the issues seemed to demand, as if they had to build up their courage to express disagreement and break out of the consensus mould. Differences that might have emerged quite straightforwardly in a secret ballot were either sent underground or else intensified into personal dispute. Meetings thus gave a false impression of harmony and agreement, or else an exaggerated impression of anger and disquiet. Either way, the more orthodox procedures of formal voting and secret ballots might have provided a fairer – and easier – representation of views.

The women's movement faced similar problems and discussed them in terms of the false unity imposed by 'sisterhood' (see, for instance, Rowbotham 1983; Phillips 1984) which made it peculiarly difficult for feminists to disagree. The presumption of a shared experience and a common interest seemed to discourage tolera- tion of difference, and it became hard to deal with conflicts of opinion as neither more nor less than that. Not that feminists had been expecting any automatic consensus or had thought that women would by definition agree. More powerfully perhaps, the notion of sisterhood reflected a sense of women as able to trans- form their perception of themselves; it carried with it the expecta- tion that whatever the attitudes, beliefs and values with which a woman first approached a women's liberation group, these would be likely to undergo radical change. A frequent image in the early years was of women throwing off layer after layer of self- deprecation, self-denial and self-hate; the very metaphor suggests an inner core, which we all reach when we are true to ourselves. To the extent that they anticipated convergence and a final and agreed destination, feminists added yet more weight to the usual pressures of a face-to-face meeting.

The fear of offending individual friends was thus compounded by the fear of offending against what ought to be shared principles and views, and the price of non-conformity could rise far too high. At different moments over the last twenty years, feminists have, of course, taken up different positions and beliefs. But at each point in time it has been hard to query the dominant views, and many women (again I have no better evidence than impressions) have spoken after the event of thoughts that they hardly dared voice even to themselves. Under the pressures to consensus, disagreements were muted, and perhaps not even admitted by people who preferred to think that everyone agreed. At the same time, there was the mirror image that Jane Mansbridge has observed. Disagreements were expressed in exaggerated hostility, as if people could not understand how others could think diffe- rently from themselves.

How much of this reflects a dynamic peculiar to feminist poli- tics, how much a more general phenomenon that will arise whe- never the meeting takes pride of place? Women's groups clearly found it hard to develop the mechanisms for coping with conflicts of interest or for achieving a compromise between alternative views. Part of this did stem from the nature of feminist politics and that sense (now substantially dissipated) that women would learn to see the ways in which their interests were fundamentally shared. The liberalism in liberal democracy usually starts from the opposite direction: assuming that people and their interests are fixed and given, that they can be counted but will not be changed. The weakness in this is that it does not allow for the many ways in which we can modify and develop our positions; the strength, however, is that it accepts disagreement as inevitable – and certainly not anyone's fault. Radical politics often verges on the illiberal, just because the beliefs matter so much. For the women's movement, which explicitly challenged the distinction between personal and political and fused lifestyle with politics in an excitingly explosive mix, this tendency was even harder to avoid.

The women's movement relied not only on face-to-face meetings, but more specifically on a network of small groups. This aspect further limits the lessons that can be derived from feminist experience. In principle, for example, it is perfectly feasible to combine face-to-face meeting with formal votes and secret ballots, so that even if people are intimidated from voicing their views, they can still register their anonymous dissent. It is in smaller gatherings that this option is least available, for the enhanced intimacy brings its own constraints. Where everyone knows everyone else, it can be difficult to challenge a consensus, and the seemingly innocent request for a formal vote becomes an antagonistic act. Many will recognize this pressure from workplace meetings or committees. It is the frequent practice for the person chairing the meeting to sum up 'the mood of the meeting', and it is considered at the least gauche, at the most hostile, to nonetheless insist on a vote. Because of this, people often discover too late that a majority was in fact opposed to the 'agreed' result; each had thought herself in a minority and so gave no voice to an alternative point of view.

In larger gatherings it will be less stressful to insist on a formal vote, and indeed this is more often just a standard part of proceedings. Everyone present will then be enfranchised, but the result may still not reflect the majority's concerns. A continuing difficulty is that those who are reluctant or unable to argue in the meeting lose their opportunity for influencing others; those more adept in discussion are able to steer the debate. Meeting-based decisions will always be weighted towards those who know how to talk, and while part of this may be considered legitimate, some of it is surely unfair. People may perhaps see some justification in a process that gives additional weight to those who have thought more deeply and clearly about issues – and anyway, short of eliminating all communication and discussion, it is impossible for this not to occur. But the unequal weighting is less defensible where it derives simply from a facility in argument or a confidence in public speaking; or where the acquiescence of the silent majority stems from the fear of appearing foolish or the fear of giving offence.

The small informal groups of the women's liberation movement can claim considerable success in dealing with the first of these fears. The atmosphere of mutual support enabled many women to speak in meetings for the first time, with a growing confidence that they had something to say. The greater the success on this score, however, the greater the difficulty on the other, for the very intimacy and informality that helps dissipate the fear of making a fool of oneself can be precisely what increases the fear of giving offence. It seems almost endemic to the pursuit of democracy that the principles we dream up as a solution to one aspect turn up new problems of their own. In this case, the women's movement breached the barriers between politics and friendship, and in the informality of its small group discussions made it much easier for women to voice their thoughts and participate in collective decisions. This, however, set up new obstacles to open discussion, acting in some cases to censor differences of opinion, in others to intensify dispute. Because it had divergent effects, it would be dishonest to use the more unfortunate of the consequences as a definitive argument against the attempt. But clearly there are multiple consequences to every 'democratic' procedure, and we need to understand these in the choices we make.

Securing accountability and open decisions The same sense of going one step forward, two steps back haunts the problem of accountability, and this was the major theme of Jo Freeman's 1970 pamphlet on *The Tyranny of Structurelessness* and her later book on *The Politics of Women's Liberation* (1975). Freeman argues that all organizations have their procedures for making decisions, and that when a group claims to be without them, it is evading the crucially democratic task of keeping such procedures under control. According to the ideal, all the women in a women's group were equals: all equally able to influence decisions, none taking on a leading or dominant role. The reality was often quite different, for those who knew one another best had a tremendous hidden advantage. They talked to one another outside of meetings, form-ing a (perhaps unconscious) caucus that then shaped general discussion. Once in the meeting, they listened to each other with particular sympathy, making it more difficult for 'outsiders' to speak. Their powerful sense of shared assumptions, jokes and references sustained them but made difficulties for others, and created a hidden structure of power. The problem with power that is based on friendship networks is that it does not look like power, and is therefore rarely brought to account. Power that is acknow-ledged can be subjected to mechanisms of democratic control; power that is denied can become unlimited and capricious.

The most widely discussed aspect of Jo Freeman's intervention was her analysis of what feminists termed the 'star' system. Most women's groups operated without any structure of formal repre-sentation and did not elect women to speak for the group. Journal-ists found this impossible to deal with and just adopted their own preferred stars. The women who were picked as 'leading lights' and asked for interviews or to appear on TV could ultimately only speak for themselves. There had been no discussion to settle the line they should take, and they were not subject to any means of control. Many nonetheless attempted to 'represent' what they saw as the movement's view, but when they found themselves increasingly the focus of other women's resentment and com-plaint, they sometimes reacted in the most outrageous of ways. Excess criticism broke the links, and the stars drifted into a world of their own.

Freeman's argument has most purchase on what happened in the USA in the late 1960s and early 1970s, where there was considerable media interest in the emergent women's movement. In Britain, by contrast, there was no great rush to create feminist 'stars'. But a later version of the same argument raises similar points. By the 1980s, there was considerable dissatisfaction over the women who had become 'experts' on the movement, either as writers or on the academic terrain. Again, there was a feeling that these women had broken with the principles of women's move-ment democracy in letting themselves be taken up as stars; again, there was a feeling that they misrepresented the movement, giving just their own individual views. Jo Freeman would presum-ably make the same response as she did to the argument about media stars: a movement which refuses to choose its own spokes-women, or to formalize procedures for ensuring that they say what they should, is not in much of a position to complain.

Spokeswomen, experts, stars there will be, so at least choose the ones that you want, and then bring them under some kind of control.

The point about friendship networks was well taken in subsequent feminist discussion, and it was widely accepted that there were hidden structures of power. The usual response, unfortunately, was to redouble efforts at non-hierarchical forms, the risk being that this presented any shortcomings as essentially an individual's fault. With the chimera of a purely egalitarian democracy still holding sway, the gaps between theory and practice get interpreted as a failure of will, and a damaging cycle of accusation, resentment and guilt can be the unhappy result. (Many women felt that this was indeed their experience.) The alternative reaction is that recommended by numerous writers on democracy: to accept that there is always a hierarchy of power, and try to make the leaders accountable to the led.

As Freeman insists, this second route need not involve total capitulation to the dull and disheartening techniques of representative democracy. There is a host of mechanisms through which organizations can hope to reduce their internal hierarchy and maximize participation and control. These include agreeing precise guidelines on what the spokeswomen or 'leaders' can do; insisting on regular report-backs; and setting time limits on the period any one person can hold office. But such mechanisms only come into play once organizations acknowledge there is a problem. The more utopian the version of democracy, in other words, the more potentially authoritarian the outcome – not because utopians are any worse than the rest of us, but because they do not adequately protect themselves against what cynics will anticipate as inevitable results.

This is not an unfamiliar view: it constitutes the theme tune of minimalist democracy. I am considerably more sympathetic to it than I used to be, and more sympathetic than when I began on this book. In the case of the women's movement, however, women got together for more than making decisions, and what happened was a trade-off between accountability and other concerns. Jane Mansbridge makes the point that it is only in the context of conflicting interests that we begin to worry about the niceties of political equality. In a working environment where people share the same basic interests and concerns, for example, they will not necessarily bother about having numerically equal power. In the same way, the kind of accountability that preoccupies Jo Freeman is not always appropriate or important, and too much emphasis on bringing people to book can prove destructive when interests and priorities do not really diverge. The difficulty, of course, is knowing when it does matter, and if minimalist democracy errs on the side of caution (assuming that a division will always emerge between leaders and led), many strands of participatory democracy stand accused of the opposite fault.

Membership and representation In considering the arguments for an increased representation of women in national and local politics, I outlined two different meanings that we attach to representation. One deals with the mirror effect and focuses on the extent to which organizations have reflected the different identities and groupings into which we divide; the other concentrates on the proportional representation of opinions and ideas. The women's movement could not seriously claim to represent women in either sense. With neither membership cards nor elections, neither delegates nor representative structure, it could not say for whom or how many it spoke. Most of the time this is no problem, for as long as feminism is about challenging and transforming received practice or ideas, it does not have to claim to be a representative body. It is when feminists seek an increasingly direct impact in the policy arena that representation becomes a thorny concern.

In the earliest years of the movement, women were defiantly unrepresentative, knowing full well that what they stood for was something most women would reject. 'The world will not change overnight,' urged Germaine Greer, 'and liberation will not happen unless individual women agree to be outcasts, eccentrics, perverts, and whatever the powers-that-be choose to call them' (1971: 328). Most feminists were sustained by the belief that their vision would ultimately be shared, but none would have claimed that she 'represented' what a majority currently believed. Women knew from their own experiences how powerful were the forces to conformity, how difficult it could be to break ranks. So when the women's movement provoked angry reaction over what 'real' women 'really' wanted, or fierce denunciations of the feminists as a misguided and misleading few, this was all as expected or even – occasionally – as desired. It was an act of some impudence to describe this gathering of outcasts and rebels as 'the women's movement' – but if that sparked interest and debate, what more could one hope to achieve?

The other aspect of representation produced greater anxiety, though here again was a sense of defying previous concerns. Feminists noted, for example, that middle-class women pre-dominated in those joining the movement, and from early in the 1970s, some women were questioning the ways in which their dominance was maintained. But it was also characteristic of these earlier years that women gloried in having released themselves from the preoccupations of a purely socialist politics and in having claimed their freedom to say that women faced oppression regard-less of their position and class (see Phillips 1987a:ch. 5). Once race became a major issue, however, the lack of proportionality had to be admitted as a more serious affair. Class had been too much tainted by neanderthal socialists who saw in feminism only a bourgeois concern. Race had no parallel history, and when femin-ists were finally brought to acknowledge the dominance of white women – in the USA, this dates from the late 1970s, in Britain, the early to mid 1980s, in some parts of Europe, the process has barely begun – there was no such easy way to dismiss the evidence or describe it as beside the point. The (always shaky) perception of women as sharing common concerns was then extensively con-tested, as was the notion that feminism meant a unified set of globally appropriate demands. (There has been a lengthy litera-ture on this, but see, for example, Carby 1982; Smith 1983; Mohanty 1989.) Once the unity of 'woman' is shattered, it begins to matter who the feminists are.

The same question has arisen in the very different context of lobbying over policies and power. Once women's groups edged towards a role in public policy, or began to campaign within political parties and unions for an increased representation of women, they were called on to indicate the constituency from which they came. They could not afford to be dismissed as eccentric footnotes or the peculiar expression of an extraordinary few; they needed to say for how many they spoke and for whom. There are no obvious mechanisms for doing this other than the conventional ones of counting the members and recording their votes. Any group can campaign, but once it claims for itself some role in decisions, it has to deal with the problems of representa-tion.

Many of the relevant examples are about women's groups

seeking to change governmental policy through lobbying and pressure group activities, but there are also cases that deal with women in elected roles. The recent experience of the Icelandic Women's Party is particularly interesting here. Kwenna Frambothid (KF–strictly Women's List) was formed in 1981 out of a coalition of women's groups, and contested the city council elections in the following year (Styrkarsdottir 1986). After impressive successes in the two major towns of Akureyri and Reykjavik, the KF councillors adopted contrasting strategies, in the first case joining a left of centre governing coalition, in the second trying to sustain a more direct action approach from outside. The Reykjavik KF determined to maintain a forum through which the women who had been so involved in the election campaign could continue to influence the two women elected, hoping thereby to generate forms of representation and accountability that would extend beyond the ballot box norm. Weekly meetings were organized in which the two councillors outlined issues that were due to arise in council and sought advice and feedback over what they should do.

The experiment was not a great success. Weekly meetings dwindled into fortnightly meetings, and by 1985–6 only six or so 'tired and disillusioned women' (Dominelli and Jonsdottir 1988: 52) were still keeping the momentum going. The reasons were complex, for the difficulties faced by any forum that relies on a high-level contribution of energy and time were in this case grafted on to further difficulties generated by the conventions of the political process. Participatory and representative democracy were trying to work in tandem, and the combination did not work too well.

> Contributing to their disenchantment was the fact that the meetings seldom allowed space for women to cover anything other than council matters. The pressures of time inhibited discussion so that even when considering council items, the lengthy agendas necessitated the guillotining of debates on issues of major import to women. As these meetings became of less interest and relevance, women's participation in them declined and KF councillors soon found themselves having to take decisions and formulate policy without a mandated position from their supporters. (Dominelli and Jonsdottir 1988:44)

The meetings were not only tiny, but very unrepresentative: the 'tyranny of domestic commitments' (p. 40) virtually barred working-class women.

These and other examples pose serious questions about direct versus representative democracy, but, of course, the reasons why Kwenna Frambothid wanted more continuous communication between supporters and councillors still stand. And if we compare the experience of the women's movement with that of conventionally representative bodies, we can see some of what is at stake. The women's movement was not representative but it had so many other more positive sides. The fact that women did not 'join' in any formalized way meant the impact of feminism was considerably wider than the numbers who went to conferences or groups, for by reading, thinking, talking and trying to change their own personal lives, women could feel that they were also part of this 'movement'. The fact that any woman who found out about a conference or centre or group could just go along made it possible to drift in without yet being sure what it was all about. This had its disadvantages (it was equally easy to drift out) but was probably crucial to the development of a movement that began as a mystery to most women outside. Because there was no formal difference between the woman who came on her own and the woman who came from a group, or between the woman who had just arrived and the woman who had been there from the start, there was less of that deadening sense of everything being settled in advance by those who were in the know. Instead of feeling swallowed up in a bureaucracy, women felt they were joining something that did indeed move.

Compare this with the more familiar experiences of joining a party or union or pressure group. A membership card arrives through the post, followed (when the system works) by occasional details of future meetings. The meetings are as often as not obscurely laden with incomprehensible acronyms; motions are debated and forwarded to heaven knows where. All political groups can be daunting to the newcomer, and we have already seen that feminists were unhappy with the women's movement record on this. But this was failing to live up to a very high standard: other organizations did not even begin to meet it. The conventions of representation are flawed in a variety of ways, and anyone who has studied party or trade union conferences will tell tales of the behind-the-scenes dealings in which delegation A agrees to cast its votes behind delegation B and extracts some appropriate return. The good side to this is that the weight accorded to the two delegations reflects the number of people they represent. The bad side is that those numbers become trading counters, in a mere parody of democratic choice and control.

That the women's movement could not legitimately claim to 'represent' women seems to me one of the lesser of its problems, though where it incorporated into its politics the priorities and even prejudices of a distinct subgroup, this was rightly a cause for concern. But many of the ways in which organizations claim to speak for their members are highly suspect, and while a movement that has *no* mechanism for establishing its representativeness will be more open than most to criticism, it is not the role of each and every organization to establish precise numerical representation. Indeed, on this issue, I consider the argument that other organizations should learn from the women's movement considerably stronger than its opposite – and would say that this process has already begun. Many organizations now take more seriously than before, for example, the question of how to make meetings more welcoming to newcomers. They try to reduce bureaucratic barriers between member and group, to curb the formalities of the agenda and to let people feel there is something they can do. The women's movement can take much of the credit for these efforts towards greater accessibility and informality.

Unlike some of the previous points then, the question of representation is not so much a problem for the women's movement itself. It arises only in terms of how far the kind of participatory democracy practised by feminists can serve as a model for the polity as a whole. At one level, it clearly cannot. In any sizeable state, there must be procedures for representation, and these should give due weight to each constituent, not more to those who make the loudest noise. This is barely in question: no one is proposing to eliminate the vote. But at an intermediate level, the choice between direct and representative forms remains, and it points us towards the final issue – the role and place of the meeting.

The role of decision-making by meeting The obvious point about meetings is that most people do not attend. If non-attenders were distributed at random through all the divisions in society – the same proportions of each race, class and sex, the same proportions across a spectrum of beliefs – this would be no great cause for concern. We might express some regret that so many people find politics a drag, but their absence would make little difference to the results, and we could still say these were democratically achieved. Almost invariably, however, the opposite is true. Those who find the time, energy, commitment and confidence to attend meetings are not a representative group.

One of the episodes in Jane Mansbridge's Vermont town is particularly revealing here. One might have thought a single annual town meeting would not make too much of a demand, and that attendance might therefore prove more representative than most. In fact there was a definite pattern of involvement and power, and it was skewed to 'the old-timers, those who live in the village, the middle classes, the men, and the old' (1980:89). On issues over which there were no significant conflicts of interests, this did not much matter, but on others it could be all-important. In 1969 the big question was the education budget. The costs of the school had risen steeply, and the town meeting rejected the proposed budget which would have increased local taxation. A special meeting was then convened to deal with the problem. This time, because of strenuous efforts by the school board to get as many parents as possible to attend, the budget was passed and taxes were raised. Critics complained that the second meeting had been 'packed'. In one sense this was undoubtedly true, for people who had never previously attended town meetings were encouraged by the school to come along for the very first time. Yet, when Mansbridge compared those who attended with the community as a whole, on most of the key divisions – by class, age, whether people had children at school, whether they were old-timers or newcomers, lived in the village or further away – it was the second meeting that was the representative one.

> Very rarely, as in the May 1969 meeting, an almost representative body may gather in town meetings to make decisions for the town. But such equal representation is achieved only by an extraordinary effort to offset the usual communications networks and the usual disparate balance of incentives. Otherwise, year in and year out, the decisions of the town are made in a body that in moments of conflict systematically misrepresents the conflicting interests of the towns-people. (p. 114)

Meetings become representative only under exceptional conditions. A postal ballot might produce fairer results.

To one of the complaints levelled at meeting-based democracy – that people cannot deal with the demands on their time – the women's movement has a partial response. When politics is all-involving, then people will participate more actively and intensely than one could have imagined possible. 'The costs of participation, of which some make so much, do not feel heavy (Mansbridge 1980:9). On the question of the extent to which the meeting can reflect adequately and proportionately all the relevant concerns, the women's movement has no answer at all. The position women occupy in contemporary societies is one that (a) discourages women from participating equally in meetings that are open to both women and men; and (b) discourages the majority of women from the intense involvement that a women's movement can mean. The difficulties women experience in getting to and staying at meetings are all too well known, and the double shift is such a familiar phenomenon that it has entered into everyday speech. Any feminist sociology will highlight this problem of time, and this factor alone would seem to designate meeting-based democracy as necessarily biased in favour of men.

Yet the women's movement took participation almost as its definition of democracy, and I can think of no feminist theorist who waxes enthusiastic in the alternative vein. This might be thought an extraordinary case of mistaken identity, but it has its roots in two other features of women's position. The first will be clear by now, for it has been noted in a number of sections. Because women have so often internalized their subordination, they need active participation and discussion if they are to be able to transform and recreate themselves. If women's interests were a simple 'given', it would be a matter of ensuring them an adequate voice and making their influence proportional to their numbers. Instead of the given, however, women have often talked of discovery, even to the point of having to 'discover' that they were oppressed. Jean Grimshaw describes how 'a remark which might once have been seen as complimentary or flattering is now seen as patronizing or demeaning' and observes that 'sexism begins to appear endemic and endless' (1986:80). This may sound odd, but it is precisely what many women have experienced – a sea-change in perceptions where things once accepted as just part of existence reappear as insulting, controlling and unfair. Benjamin Barber has linked the belief that interests are pre-given with the minimal democracy of the vote, and the belief that interests get transformed with strong democracy, participation and talk. Notwithstanding the reservations expressed by Iris Young, the women's movement made the same connection.

The other thing that keeps feminists attached to participatory models is women's seclusion inside the home. This is a more contentious point, both because women are less defined through the private, household sphere than in the past, and because feminists have taken such varied positions on how to respond to the seclusion that remains. There is, for example, a continuing and lively debate on whether feminists should campaign for full and equal acceptance within the world of work or for a revaluation of women's traditional sphere, and the idea that women must be liberated *from* the home is not universally shared. In two influential but also representative contributions, Betty Friedan, for example, has covered both ends of the spectrum. In 1963 she wrote *The Feminine Mystique*, which focuses on the wasted lives of women confined to the home and their famous 'problem with no name'; in *The Second Stage* (1981) she produced what was in effect an auto-critique, arguing against the illusory liberation that was turning working women into surrogate men. In much of the current feminist literature, there is an increasing focus on sexual difference, sometimes as a glorification of the supposedly female values, other times, less contentiously, as a reminder that some difference will always remain. Some of the arguments (as in Jean Bethke Elshtain's position on the family) lead in a conservative direction; others (like Zillah Eisenstein's discussion of employment equality) take a more radical, innovative route. On questions of democracy, however, the older arguments seem to be retaining their strength. Politics is almost by definition a matter of engaging with other people and other concerns, and it does not fit with being private or contained.

One measure of this is that no feminist (to my knowledge) takes any interest in the scenarios for 'computer democracy'. Sarah Perrigo, for example, finds 'those technocratic utopias that would have all of us working from home and pressing buttons to participate in "democratic" decisions extremely unattractive' (1988). Yet in many ways this might have appeared as a feminist ideal. The information revolution is creating the conditions for wide-ranging and almost continuous referendums and, setting aside for the moment the costs, could in principle link each household into national networks relaying continually updated political information on to television screens. Interactive technology makes it possible for people to put questions from their homes to politicians in studios and to register an instant national vote. When alternative visions of participatory democracy have been so much weighted towards the male workplace, or have called for an almost impossible investment of time, this might look like the answer to every woman's dream. At last a scenario that eliminates the sexual inequalities and transcends the barriers between public and private spheres.

There are, of course, problems with this vision of democracy, and Giovanni Sartori regards the whole thing with horror and disdain:

> daily direct democracy in which the citizenry sits before a video and allegedly self-governs itself by responding to the issue in the air by pressing a button. How nice – and how deadly . . . The idea that the government of our fantastically complex, interconnected and fragile societies could be entrusted to millions of *discrete wills* that are bound to decide *at random*, with a *zero–sum instrument* – this idea is indeed a monumental proof of the abyss of under-comprehension that is menacing us. (1987:247)

Referendum democracy could remove what protection now exists for minority rights. Politics, Sartori argues, is about negotiations, trade-offs and coalitions, and in this process minorities get some benefits even when outvoted in numerical terms. Governments are always constrained by the opposition, which might itself become government next time; instead of capitalizing on their current monopoly of power, they offer trade-offs to strengthen future position. Referendums, by contrast, mean treating each decision as separate and absolute: anyone unfortunate enough to be in the (possibly large) minority would have no compensatory pressure or power. 'Not only majority rule would become absolute or unlimited, but no trade-offs, no compensations, could occur among issues either. Since every referendum-type decision is a discrete and self-contained decision, it cannot be tempered by "exchanges", by cross-issue adjustments or corrections (not even if required on the grounds of consistency)' (p. 115).

This is a pertinent point and, from his opposite perspective, Benjamin Barber also voices concern about electronic balloting as 'soliciting instant votes' (1984:290). But these are not the main sources of feminist indifference, which stem more directly from a continuing anxiety over women's seclusion in the home. All the forms of democracy that feminists have explored have been ones that would counteract the passivity and isolation that is so often a woman's experience, and despite acute difficulties over time, a vision of increased and public participation constantly reappears. The problems can seem almost overwhelming, but there is no way of dislodging participation from feminist dreams. However difficult, this is seen as the way forward.

One theme that has recurred through this chapter is that when the ideals of democratic equality are set impossibly high, they can produce contradictory effects. The radical egalitarianism that rotated group responsibilities and tried to equalize everyone's involvement in discussion did reduce hierarchy, but it also increased irritability and often led to mutual recrimination. The emphasis on talking things through rather than just taking a vote did enable women to rethink and develop their ideas, but also made conflicts more difficult to acknowledge and resolve. The resistance to formal structures did help counter the divisions into leaders and led, but also made accountability an impossible task. The absence of any system of membership did make the movement more accessible and open, more informal and thus – for some women – easier to join, but it also limited any representational claims. The central role played by the meeting did mean women's engagement was more direct and intense, but also limited this to those able to attend.

The recent experience of the women's movement is in many ways discouraging. It suggests that we cannot have everything we want, and certainly not all at the same time. There seem to be no procedures, mechanisms or scenarios that will satisfactorily meet all possible conditions or visions of democracy, and though many writers have treated this as a problem of competing definitions, it has its more substantive side. The choices people make for increasing one kind of democratic equality can potentially undermine another – but then as long as this is acknowledged, it can be built into the decisions people take. The difficulties arise more from the ways in which groups respond when they discover that democracy is not so easy. In the case of the women's movement, the worst outcome has been when failures have been regarded as somebody's fault, and women have been felt to be failing to live up to their ideals. When individuals are held personally to account, this generates an unhappy atmosphere of mutual distrust – which cannot be what democracy requires. Neither, of course, is the opposite extreme. In any organization, individuals should assume some responsibility for the degree of democracy that is achieved, not dismiss all problems as 'society's fault' and postpone democracy to some better, future world. One of the arts of democracy is working out the extent to which we *are* responsible, but without presuming we have ultimate and complete control. Since this is one of the classic problems of the human condition, it is not surprising to discover it here.

The other typical response to the contradictions and tensions of democracy is to give it all up as an impossible job. It is one of the more unfortunate consequences of radical egalitarianism that it can so disillusion its supporters when the ambitions are not after all met. There is a common trajectory, followed, for example, by Robert Michels. He began with active involvement in the German socialist movement; he ended with the view that democracy produced oligarchy and could, in its full sense, be no more than a dream (see his *Political Parties*, written in 1911 – Michels 1962). The experience of radical democracy often turns into an argument for the most minimal and cautious approach, and this should serve as salutary warning to those who set their ideals of democracy too high. It is no argument, however, against working to improve what we have.

The final theme that has surfaced through this discussion is that where there are differences of opinion and conflicts of interest, societies must ultimately rely on the procedures of political equality, which in the end means the ballot box and elections. The more participatory versions of democracy potentially founder on the problems of guaranteeing to everyone an equal weight, which is why meeting-based involvement and participation can never substitute for the equal right to vote. With all the undoubted inadequacies, no one has come up with a satisfactory alternative device, and all efforts towards increasing participation must continue to be an adjunct to this. This is not a dramatic new point, for many have stressed the false opposition between direct and representative democracy (for example, Mansbridge 1980; Bobbio 1984; Held 1986; Keane 1988a) and pointed out that whatever conclusions we reach on extending or deepening democracy, these should not be presented as alternatives to representation.

6

SO WHAT'S WRONG WITH
LIBERAL DEMOCRACY?

One of the difficulties in coming to terms with liberal democracy is that those who challenge a consensus usually get the cleverest lines, while those who defend what is taken for granted slide into common-sense argument and fall down on intellectual appeal. The centuries-old confrontation between liberalism and its critics seems to exemplify this rule. Compared to the alternatives, the liberal tradition has had a pretty easy ride in the Western democracies, and though its more rigorous exponents can point to an accumulation of ways in which the practice is inferior to the theory, liberalism generally occupies the central ground. Perhaps because of this, its supporters have sometimes put their case in the most uninspiring of ways. There are occasional flights of the imagination which lend to the liberal tradition the flavour of grand theory: most recently Fukuyama (1989), who puts the political successes of liberalism in an ambitiously Hegelian framework, and proclaims the end of history as a result. More often, however, liberalism draws its strength from the fact that it *is* common, and that therefore it makes the most sense.

Those who find liberalism wanting have developed impressively powerful critiques, and to anyone with a taste for theoretical argument, they offer considerably more satisfying fare. Usually prefacing their alternatives with a careful analysis of liberalism's assumptions and faults, their insights have been imaginative and astute. The defendants do not always respond in kind. Karl

Popper (1945), for example, dropped far below his usual standards of rigour when criticizing Hegel and Marx, and relied on hearsay as much as textual analysis. Others have been content to sprinkle their rebuttals with easy reference to totalitarian society or contemptuous nods at utopian dreams, and have not bothered with systematic refutation. The contest has thus been uneven, with the complacencies of common sense on one side and the intricacies of theory on the other; while liberal democracy has triumphed in the realm of political practice, it cannot claim to have won the battle of ideas. Though challenged from a variety of angles – including, in this book, feminist, republican and participatory – liberalism rarely bothers to be so clever.

This creates an imbalance in the debates, and the very ingenuity of the alternatives may make them look more substantial than they are. Karl Marx's *On The Jewish Question*, for example, written in 1843, has been a reference point for many analyses of the liberal tradition and, with its striking contrasts between the heavenly universality of liberal citizenship and the grubby exploitations of the private sphere, has set the agenda for many later critiques (Marx and Engels 1975). Yet the alternative Marx developed has not proved satisfactory, and while his conception of freedom is still widely felt to be 'far deeper and richer than negative or classical liberal views' (Lukes 1985:149), his notion of democracy remains utopian or vague. Carried away by the power of the analysis, people have not always paused to consider all the consequences; this failure has left Marxism profoundly defensive in the face of recent democratic revolutions.

The point is not that critics must develop a fully fledged alternative before it is possible to judge the validity of their critique: if we were to set this as the standard there would be little scope for the development of ideas. Feminism has been seen as adding decisive weight to the charges against liberal democracy, and has viewed this tradition as peculiarly resistant to gender concerns. Yet as Carole Pateman rightly observes in her conclusion to *The Sexual Contract*:

> To retrieve the story of the sexual contract does not, of itself, provide a political programme of offer any short cuts in the hard task of deciding what, in any given circumstances, are the best courses of action and policies for feminists to follow, or when and how feminists should form alliances with other political movements. Once the story has been told, however, a new perspective is available from

which to assess political possibilities . . . When the repressed story of political genesis is brought to the surface, the political landscape can never look the same again. (1988:233)

Gender does and should change the way we think about democracy, but given the pervasive power of existing traditions, it will be some time before the details of the new landscape become clear. We should not too easily presume, however, that all of the features will change.

From individuals to groups Among the issues that have emerged in feminist theory, the most provocative centre around universality. A number of recent contributions query the notion that democracy means being treated the same and challenge the idea that citizens must leave their bodies – hence their selves – behind when they enter the public arena. As Carole Pateman, Zillah Eisenstein, Iris Marion Young and others have argued, there *is* no gender-neutral individual, and when liberals try to deal with us only in our capacity as abstract citizens, they are wishing away not only differences of class but what may be even more intransigent differences of sex. Liberal democracy wants to ignore (and civic republicanism to transcend) all more local identities and difference; in reality both traditions have insinuated the male body and male identity into their definitions of the norm. Liberal democrats, in particular, believed they had extended all necessary rights and freedoms to women when they allowed them to vote on the same terms as men. This is quite simply inadequate, as even the crudest of indicators (like the number of women in politics) will show. Democracy cannot stand above sexual difference but has to be reconceptualized with difference firmly in mind. One obvious implication is that democracy must deal with us not just as individuals but groups.

I think this is right, and any argument for an enhanced representation of women in politics relies on some such view. The composition of our elected assemblies matters because people are not all the same, and the fact that it is so consistently skewed towards certain categories and groups is evidence enough for this point. When the characteristics of those elected deviate to any significant degree from those of the electorate as a whole, there is a clear case for saying something is wrong. These 'characteristics' have obviously proved themselves relevant, and some groups have become more powerful than the rest.

Up to this point, of course, many liberals will be prepared to agree. Liberals have a good record on issues of discrimination – sometimes better than their more radical critics – and most will express satisfaction when more women or people from ethnic minorities are elected. The best of liberals, however, still find it hard to switch their thinking to groups. The anti-discrimination that informs much contemporary liberalism implies removing obstacles that block an individual's path and then applauding when that individual succeeds. The problem is still perceived in terms of previous *mis*treatment, which judged and dismissed people because they had deviated from some prejudiced norm. The answer is presented in terms of treating them just as people instead.

The continuing tension between those who argue for equal opportunities and those who stress the importance of affirmative action is one example of the gap between liberal anti-discrimination and the mechanisms that would actively ensure an equal representation of women. As soon as the argument moves into the realm of mechanisms and guarantees then it challenges some of the founding principles of liberal democracy. At a practical level this concerns the free choice of party selectorates. The idea of guaranteed seats for women, or 40 per cent quotas for either sex, inevitably circumscribes the freedom of those who are selecting candidates and, to this extent if no other, comes into conflict with liberal ideals. More fundamentally, however, any measure that is designed to ensure an increased representation of women is saying that sexual difference is politically relevant, and that democracy must recognize groups. Moving beyond the notion of fair-dos for women (improving their access, if they want it, to political careers), it says that our assemblies are unrepresentative whenever they are skewed to one sex. Once we move on to the terrain of mechanisms, as we surely must, we are dealing explicitly with difference and acknowledging it as a political concern.

Leaving aside the option that advises us to carry on regardless, there are only two serious approaches to women's under-representation. The first extends but can be made compatible with liberal democratic thinking. It identifies additional obstacles to political involvement that too many people had hitherto ignored, including, for example, the working hours and conditions of councils and assemblies, the prejudices and conventions through which parties select their candidates and, in the case of the USA, the absurd amount of money candidates are expected to spend. Where any of these conditions can be shown to discriminate specifically against women candidates, the barriers must be reduced or removed. This argument may be pushing liberal democracy to its limits, for it introduces matters that used to be thought of as personal or private concerns. As long as it is about removing barriers, however, and not yet dictating the eventual result, it is in tune with liberal ideals. It means women will no longer be actively kept out, but it leaves it up to them as individuals whether they seize on their new opportunities for involvement.

The second alternative refuses to take this risk and, as in the strategies recently adopted by various political parties, writes in procedures that will ensure a more balanced result. People frequently debate these two alternatives as if they reflect just different degress of determination for change: the first, a pious resolution that removes barriers but will almost certainly leave things as before; the second, a more dedicated commitment that understands the strength of resistance to women's representation and knows that only guarantees will alter the results. This is one element in the argument, but the political underpinnings are also notably different. The first approach continues to regard us in our character as abstract individuals and concentrates on reducing the relevance of our sex. The second approach recognizes that society is composed of different groups, and that these groups may develop different interests. Because of this, it will not leave proportionality to chance. The first approach says it should not matter whether we are women or men, and that we should make sure procedures are genuinely neutral; the second says the sexes have different degrees of power, and that the distribution must therefore be made equal.

Despite my reservations over what the 'representation of women' can mean, the second alternative is the one argued for in this book. The liberal canon insists that differences between us should not matter, but in societies driven by group interests, it is dishonest to pretend we are the same. My own vision of a desirable future is in fact unfashionably androgynous, and I look forward to a time when we are treated as people, no longer as women or men. But it is one thing to wish for this future and quite another to wish differences away. The economic and political structures of contemporary societies exhibit a high degree of sexual and racial segregation, and where there are definable groups, there are inevitably group interests. One principle that should therefore inform the practices of a democracy is that representatives should mirror the sexual, racial and, where relevant, national composition of the society as a whole, and that there should be mechanisms to achieve this effect. Such proportionality would be automatic if there were no vested interests and no structures sustaining group power: as long as the numbers elected were large enough, the principles of random selection would be enough to achieve proportional results. That they have never yet done so demonstrates the need for change. When one group is consistently under-represented, some other group is getting more than its share.

The mirror principle can, of course, be extended to other divisions, and it is part of the nature of politics that people will argue about the relevant groups. The most obvious ones to start with are those which have a biological foundation, for there is no argument that could legitimately link people's sex or race with their suitability for the political stage. If women are not elected in much the same proportions as men, and Africans or Asians not elected in broad proportion to their numbers in the electorate as a whole, then something fishy is going on (fishy but not particularly obscure). The more difficult question is how far to extend the emphasis on groups. The strongest alternative to the abstraction of the individual is to consider people *only* in their highly specified, differentiated identities: as women or men; as black or white; as worker or employer. (The logic could take us on to even more detailed self-definitions, as in the DJM (divorced Jewish male) or the SWF (single white female) of the lonely hearts column of the *New York Review of Books*.) This would involve a lot more than mechanisms for increasing the numbers of women elected, and considerably more, too, than Iris Young's proposal for a veto power for oppressed groups. If people were thought to exist only through their group identities, then democracy would become a matter only of group representation, and the key questions would be how to identify and represent each of these groups.

I would not want to take this route, but there are a few more differences that ought to be considered. Take, for example, that range of characteristics – nation of origin, religion, sexual orientation – that become more or less important as circumstances change. The argument from statistical probability applies here as well as anywhere else, though the evidence will be less conclusive if the group is small. (Chance alone might then explain why no one from the group was elected.) But the importance people attach to achieving proportionality along these characteristics will depend on whether they define themselves primarily in these terms, and whether they see these aspects as incidental or essential. As a rule, of course, it is when groups have experienced oppression because of their 'defining' characteristic that they do see themselves in these terms. Once this point is reached, some form of quota system seems a legitimate demand.

The practices of what is known as consociational democracy come closest to acknowledging this and build in protection for what are seen as the key social groups. The official justification is that in certain countries people can indeed be defined by one characteristic, the society being so segmented that, on every major issue that comes up, people align consistently with one group alone. Hence, in the Netherlands, government resources are typically distributed between the three major religious groupings (Catholic, Calvinist and secular) in proportion to their share of the population as a whole. This system recognizes the strength of group identity and attachment, though political parties continue to contest the elections on a wider basis, and the groups do not become a substitute for politics itself. Even when heterogeneity and group difference are more explicitly acknowledged, people are reluctant to reduce everything to this.

In those parts of Africa where there has been a history of ethnic tension and a continuing correlation between ethnicity and economic or political power, governments have sometimes developed mechanisms for ensuring each group some degree of representation. Nigeria, for example, has experimented extensively with quota systems and federal structures that devolve power to the local states, and it was the premature challenge to federalism that partly provoked the 1960s civil war. This is a context where some guarantees of proportional power are surely necessary, for where there has been systematic privileging of certain groups over others, there have to be procedures that will counter the effects. Precisely which mechanisms are most appropriate is always more difficult to settle, for whatever option is chosen, it can generate as much tension as it was meant to dissolve. Thus, on the one hand, there will be pressure to recognize more and more groups as deserving some form of quota protection (Nigeria, for example, has suffered from a proliferation of states); on the other, there will be tension between proportionality and the principles of merit. Most troubling of all is the potential conservatism, for if the hope is that religion or ethnicity will lose their political and economic significance and no longer determine people's access to income or power, then writing in guarantees is going at some point to become counterproductive. To continue with the example of Nigeria, where political parties have tended to reproduce a three-way ethnic divide, the preparations for a return to civilian rule in 1992 now treat this as the problem: the current proposal is that only two political parties will be allowed to register and compete.

These issues are too complicated for easy answers, but arguments about the under-representation of women need to consider them as possible ramifications. I have noted elsewhere that no one should be deterred from arguing for sexual equality by the *reductio ad absurdum* that proposes to extend this same principle to an infinity of conceivable groups. Some extension is, however, appropriate, and one useful working principle is that when a particular characteristic has come to matter (meaning that it substantially dictates the fortunes of the people whom it defines) then there should be some mechanisms to ensure that group's proportional representation. When the characteristic has losts its determining significance, these mechanisms should be brought to an end. The possible techniques include affirmative action or quota systems to be adopted by political parties; in the more acute cases they might also operate at the level of government, guaranteeing office in some proportion to numbers in the electorate as a whole. The obvious difficulty is knowing when something 'matters', and just how much it should matter before action begins. Iris Young's work on identifying oppressed groups (1988) goes some way towards dealing with these questions, but the problems and issues have barely begun to enter debate.

The final candidate for proportionality is class, and the mirror principle rather fudges this issue. People conventionally justify the tiny number of working-class people elected as representatives, by saying that they are not excluded because of class but because they lack the appropriate qualifications. Being involved in politics has become associated with certain skills, qualifications or expertise, and while there may be no basis for grounding these in a person's class of origin (they do not depend on who your parents were), they may well be associated with certain kinds of occupation or experience (lawyers are clever at speeches while a shop assistant may not have seen much of the world). Class, in other words, is said to be a relevant consideration, so that if the composition of elected assemblies turns out to be skewed towards one end of the class spectrum, there is a wholly innocent and defensible cause. A cause, however, can be innocent yet the effect far from just. When class structures people's interests, priorities and perceptions of the world to such a degree, it is surely a problem for democracy if all those who take the decisions come from a minority class. Aneurin Bevan believed we could only talk of full representation when the person elected 'spoke with the authentic accents of those who elected him', shared their values and was 'in touch with their realities' (quoted in Arblaster 1987: 84). There is enough truth in this (and more than enough parallel with what feminists have argued in relation to women) to justify fuller discussion and thought.

With all the candidates for group representation, there is, however, one outstanding difficulty: that there are so many groupings to which each of us might in principle belong. The poet June Jordan comments that 'every single one of us is more than whatever race we represent or embody and more than whatever gender category we fall into. We have other kinds of allegiances, other kinds of dreams' (quoted in Parmar 1989). We do not fall simply into one definition or another; more typically in politics, each of us flits through a number of identities, forming and reforming tentative alliances that may not survive the issue at hand. And just as well, for one common thread that links sexism, racism, nationalism and religious bigotry is the defining of self and others by a single characteristic and being able to see nothing more. Mostly, however, people exist within multiple identities, each of which may become dominant for a time. In some contexts people identify primarily with those of the same race; in others with those of the same sex. Sometimes it is class that forges the connections; sometimes nationality; very often it is ideals and beliefs. As I have argued elsewhere:

> We live in a class society that is also structured by gender, which means that men and women experience class in different ways, and that potential unities of class are disrupted by conflicts of gender. To put the emphasis the other way round: we live in a gender order that is also structured by class, which means that women experience their womanhood in different ways, and that their unity as women is continually disrupted by conflicts of class. Draw in race to complete the triangle and you can see how complex the geometry becomes. No one is 'just' a worker, 'just' a woman, 'just' black. The notion that our politics can simply reflect *one* of our identities seems implausible in the extreme. (1987a:12)

One implication is that while any system that claims to be democratic should be able to ensure that its representatives mirror the ethnic and sexual composition of the population, these representatives should not then be viewed as 'representing' their ethnic group or their sex. I argued in chapter 3 that it could be profoundly *un*democratic if women representatives were considered to be speaking only or even mainly for women, particularly when there are no substantial mechanisms for establishing what their 'constituents' support. I would now add to this that it is too limiting to regard either the elected or electorate as defined by one identity alone, and particularly when this is an identity that does not specify particular beliefs. Feminists are surely right to argue that people should not have to leave their sexual identities behind when they climb on to the political stage. But neither should they have to define themselves by one criterion, in this case by gender, alone.

Liberalism as a world of walls On matters of political representation, the emphasis on groups that are different as opposed to individuals who are in principle the same is an important corrective to the traditionally liberal approach, and carries with it specific implications about guaranteeing proportional representation to groups. Those who turn a blind eye to the sex of their candidates are not being as fair as they might think, for as long as societies are organized through sexual difference and each sex is assigned its own tasks, identities, responsibilities and roles, there should be mechanisms to ensure parity in the distribution of power. Since the other side to my argument is that any discrepancy between the proportion of women in the electorate and the proportion of women elected is proof enough that the society *is* sexually ordered, there will never be a moment at which this imperative loses its force. Either society treats men and women as genuine equals, in which case they will turn up in equal numbers in any forum for making decisions, or it treats them unfairly, in which case we need special arrangements to guarantee an equal presence.

This challenges and transforms some of the founding principles of liberalism, but falls short of a complete reversal. Most notably, I have not argued for group representation in the more substantial sense of people being represented only and always as groups; and I continue to think of politics as a means of discussing and representing what are varied, and individual, beliefs. I follow a similar path of moderation in my conclusions on the public/private divide. Here, too, I see liberalism facing serious attack, but not yet abandoned for an opposite extreme. Liberalism *is* peculiarly impervious to gender, and the distinctions it makes between public and private spheres are particularly well suited to maintaining women's political subordination. Arguments that play down the political relevance of the private sphere are doing their bit to keep things just as they are, for they encourage us to consider all is well despite what ought to be thought gross contradictions. Domestic tyranny, for example, is and should be seen to be thoroughly at odds with equal citizenship for, behind the facade of each having equal rights to participate and vote, it is carrying on as for centuries before these rights were conceived and won. Even in the more commonplace examples where women are 'allowed' to decide for themselves whether to attend a meeting and how to cast their vote, the fact that they are being allowed should alert us to the inconsistency in the way equal citizenship is being proposed. In the most seemingly equal of conditions, the continuing inequalities of the division of labour still condemn women to a lesser political role. Frequently excluded through lack of time or lack of confidence, they do not have an equal weight with men. Graduates of Oxford and Cambridge universities used to be entitled to two votes in general elections, and it was not till 1948 that this extraordinary qualification to the principle of one person, one vote was brought to an end. The liberal obsession with the public/private divide conceals and legitimates a still more damaging inequality of weight. Pretending as it does that equal rights to vote are all that matters, it refuses to engage with the constraints placed on women through their position in the domestic sphere.

On this issue, the politics of gender confirms the case made many times over in relation to class: that formal equality can combine easily with systematic privilege and is not on its own enough. The novelty in feminism is extending this to the household and family sphere. The domestic division of labour has direct consequences for the nature and degree of political involvement and because of this should be regarded as a *political* and not just social concern. Anyone concerned with sexual equality will argue for a major redistribution of household tasks and responsibilities so as to equalize the work of women and men; what has become clear is that this is an imperative of democracy as well. The formal equalities conceded through universal suffrage do not do what they claim they have done, for without the more substantial material changes, each woman counts as less than one. Counting as half is better than not counting at all, and no one is deprecating the importance of women's right to vote. But the point of universal suffrage is that it treats each person as of equal weight to the next: if so, that point is far from being reached.

A gendered approach to democracy therefore stresses domestic equalities as part of what balances out each person's political weight and includes this in its measure of what a democracy has achieved. Not that this would then become the only measure. I can conceive, for example, of a society that had substantially eroded the sexual division of labour but in which no one had a right to a vote, and it would be eccentric to present this as more democratic than a society where elections were the norm. But as long as the division of labour between women and men has political consequences, it has to be part of the political debate. In the lengthy exchanges between liberals and socialists, the significance of formal versus substantive equality has been contested as if it referred to property arrangements alone. One of the most basic contributions feminism makes to our thinking on democracy is to raise the curtain on that more private sphere.

There is, I have argued, a more assertive version of this, where feminists stress not just the 'political' consequences of 'private' arrangements but the relevance of democracy to every aspect of our social life. Anthony Arblaster has commented that 'in classical political thinking, "democracy" was the name not merely of a form of government but of a whole society, and it was habitually associated, by its enemies and critics as well as its friends, with the principle of social equality' (1987: 81). We have seen that this was far from true and that the most fervent advocates of social equality were only able to conceive of equality as a matter between men. But with the necessary adjustments to gender, this description captures many feminist concerns. In contemporary feminist politics, democracy is usually presented as something that should enter the fabric of *all* social relations, and certainly not be restricted to the way governments come about. Wherever there are decisions, there is an issue of democracy, and though some contexts will lend themselves to more formal procedures than others, all should be shaped by the same principles of equal respect. Those who joined the women's movement out of a prior experience in radical politics, or a partnership with a 'radical' man, have spoken repeatedly of the gap they found between theory and practice, and the way that the most seemingly progressive of democrats distinguished between public and private affairs. Where the intentions were supposedly so good, the contrasts were that much more startling. But elsewhere, too, women have continually found themselves in an implausible mixture of public equality and private subordination. An 'engendered' democracy has to query and subvert this divide.

Feminism multiplies the places within which democracy appears relevant, and then it alters the dimensions as well. 'Details' matter. This is one of the most powerful and abiding messages of the contemporary women's movement, extending beyond specifically sexual equality towards more general considerations on how people relate. Liberal democracy often seems to regard the equal right to vote as the apex of a democratic society. The broader conception that develops from an analysis of women treats it more as a cornerstone on which democracy can be built. A standard objection to liberal democracy is that it is so very minimal in its ideals: that the 'moment' of consent is too infrequent to count for much; that participation has been reduced to an almost gestural level; and that while the gesture matters (it still helps settle what the government will be) it cannot be seriously presented as decision-making or control. The emphasis on detail comes in at a different angle, stressing not so much the degree of control people have been able to establish over decisions, but whether they relate as political equals. The means, in other words, matter as much as the ends. If the supposed equality of the vote is continually undermined by patterns of patronage and subservience and condescension, then the society is not democratic.

None of these arguments fits well with the liberal tradition, and all of them take issue with the relationship between public and private spheres. Michael Walzer describes liberalism as 'a world of walls', each one of which creates a new liberty (1984:315), and he reworks this into his argument that justice is a matter of maintaining the boundaries between the spheres. Success in commerce, for example, should not carry with it any particular power in politics; excellence in intellectual endeavours should not give the right to have more than one vote. Walzer's *Spheres of Justice* (1983) captures much of what people object to in tyranny or nepotism or corruption, but the argument is also troubling, for it makes it harder to challenge the principles that might operate within each separate sphere. So maybe sex *should* dictate the division of labour in households, just so long as it does not dictate the arrangements that apply in schools? So maybe physical strength *is* an appropriate consideration, just so long as it stays limited to its own legitimate realm?

Walzer talks of the oppression of women in terms of the 'structures of kinship' (it is not clear what is included in this) being illegitimately reiterated through other distributive spheres. They affect, therefore, women's access to jobs, education and, in an earlier period, the vote. There is nothing, in other words, particularly wrong with what goes on inside the family. The problems begin when sex or 'kinship standing' stray outside their rightful domain. 'The real domination of women has less to do with their familial place than with their exclusion from all other places' (1983: 240). This is similar to the argument Jean Bethke Elshtain makes in *Public Man, Private Woman*: a woman's sex should not dictate what she does in the worlds of education or employment, but neither, however, should the principles of narrow self-interest become dominant in the familial sphere. But Elshtain does at least support some fusion or swapping of principles across the public/private divide. Walzer by contrast seems to be upholding the numerous distinctions between a plurality of separate spheres. From the perspectives of gender, the problem with this is that the walls people erect between one area and another can block the kind of parallels they might otherwise draw. Much of women's liberation has depended on taking the principles that were considered appropriate in one realm and saying they applied just as much to another. Progress has occurred precisely through breaching the wall.

Feminism has to query the separation of spheres, and on this score it has little confidence in the distinctions liberal democracy tries to make. And yet here, too, there is some accommodation that can be reached. Aside from rhetorical flourishes, few feminists have wanted to abandon all distinction, and on the issue of a woman's right to choose, many have incorporated liberal notions of what is an irreducibly private concern into their arguments for free and legal abortion. The further reservation I have noted derives from the republican rather than liberal tradition. Though feminism is often hijacked by those who dissolve differences of scale and kind into a disturbingly amorphous mess, there are crucial distinctions between being a citizen and being a nice caring person. A fully democratic society would be one in which people held one another in mutual respect and where all relationships, no matter how small or intimate the context, would be permeated by the principle that each person had equal weight. There would still be a difference of kind between the household, the workplace and the state.

All relationships can become 'political', but part of what that means is that all can become contexts in which we have to stand a bit back from ourselves. We have to be able to put our own wishes and needs in perspective, to create some momentary distance from our enthusiasms and preconceptions so as to recognize the significance of what others have to say. There is a difference between the approach we should adopt as citizens, and the more particular concerns that quite rightly preoccupy us in our everyday life. 'The democratization of everyday life' is thus fair enough as a slogan that captures the importance of democratic equality in every sphere of human existence. It is misleading if it denies all distinction between politics and everyday life. Democracy is not a matter of building blocks in which each brick is equally significant and all that matters is how many we can add. So while decision-making should be opened up and equalized in the household, the schools, the workplace, the housing estate, we should not regard this democratization of civil society as an alternative to a revitalized public life. The two must go hand in hand.

The curse of the meeting This leads towards the perennial issue: how much popular participation can any democracy handle, and just how much active citizenship does a 'revitalized' democracy require? I have argued that the sexual ordering of our societies is such that women need a politics of transformation and change, and that because their subordination enters so invidiously into the way that women perceive themselves and their needs, this sets a particularly high premium on discussion and talk. Liberal democracies work on the basis of limited and occasional participation, and voters are normally asked to choose between two or more vaguely defined parties, wrapped round in blandly expressed views. It is no coincidence that this finds its most dedicated supporters among those who resist radical change. Isolated voting dampens down the political imagination; in meetings, by contrast, we might begin to conceive of a wider range of options and test out our potential power. People change their views in the course of meeting and discussion, and not just because they get carried away by the enthusiasm of others and agree to things they do not truly believe. The change can be and frequently is 'real'. Vague dissatisfactions find a clearer expression, while things previously thought inevitable begin to look open to reform.

The politics of gender adds its weight to those who see isolated voting as offering too little scope for influencing the agenda and introducing new kinds of concerns. For any group that has been defined out of the mainstream of politics, this is an especially pertinent complaint. Women cannot (as women) get much purchase on a system that asks them only to register support or disapproval for existing parties or programmes. It may be that none of the alternatives has any proposals for women's specific concerns; and women may not be able even to formulate their interests without a forum in which they can talk.

When this is linked to the additional problems of women's relative domestic seclusion, feminism points towards a more actively participatory democracy than has been offered in the liberal norm. Yet the more participatory a democracy sets out to be, the more it discriminates between women and men. The more emphasis it places on activity and involvement, the more it tends to exaggerate the influence of those who have greater resources of education, charm or time. It is part of the sexually divided nature of contemporary society that women work longer than men, but with less variety of experience or length of time in formal education. Short of radical changes in the organization of paid and unpaid work, they will remain the ones least able to go out to meetings and least likely to make themselves heard. Liberal democracy has this one very strong point in its favour: by reducing the demands of participation to such a low level, it makes them more genuinely available to all.

In its own experiences of participatory democracy, the women's movement has uncovered additional strains. The circumstances of face-to-face democracy do not always promote open discussion, and when the ideals of democratic equality are set at too high a level, the resulting turmoil of guilt and accusation and resentment can drive people away from politics altogether. These are serious difficulties, and yet in the overall pattern of the 'problems of democracy', they do not occupy so very large a space. Many groups must go through a similar curve of experience, in which the initial enthusiasm for democratic equality and involvement leads through a phase of impatience and bitterness, into a more sober commitment to make things as democratic as is possible under the conditions of the day. I am reminded of Eduard Bernstein's comment on socialism, that the movement is everything and the final aim nothing. In the sense that a 'full' democracy can never be realized, but that we make as many approximations towards it as we can, the same thing can be said of democracy. Once this is accepted, and democracy conceived as a process instead of an impossibly elevated set of ideals, then the tensions associated with egalitarian decision-making (in a movement, party, trade union, committee, in a workplace or whatever kind of group) become more manageable. In all these, of course, we are dealing with people who are there. The real problems arise when people have not yet turned up.

The higher the demands, the less widespread the involvement. The more participatory the politics, the less accountable to those who are passive or inert. There seems to be a substantive choice that democrats continually face between the precise equalities of minimal democracy and the potential risks of more intense participation. The latter *is* in many ways utopian and unwieldy, but the greatest worry is that it can become liable to bias and produce unrepresentative results. When interests conflict, and even more commonly when a minority has captured an undue concentration of power, there is only one fair way to resolve the disputes: to weight each individual equally, and give each citizen a vote. It is not that liberal democracy has such a brilliant record on accountability for, as frequently noted in the course of this book, it operates at a shallow level of consent that may be no more than deciding which of the contenders should rule. The main claim to fame is that at least it distributes this favour equally between all.

Rethinking democracy through the perspectives of gender does not substantially alter the terms of the choice between minimal equality and increased participation, and feminism has no astonishing new insight that can change this dilemma. Feminism strengthens the case for active democracy, but also highlights the importance of giving each person her vote. On this central question of democracy, the alternatives remain very much as before. On the one hand there is 'the democracy of a cynical society' (Mansbridge 1980:18), which expects little in the way of involvement and regards self-protection as the highest of goals: a democracy that lacks ambition, that does not inspire, that gives us no moral satisfaction. Despite its worldly acumen, it never entirely displaces the alternatives, whose ideals reappear in every age. These counter-ideals, however, bring their own discontents in their train.

My resolution follows the kind of 'mixed economy' that has become the fashion of our day. Democracy means people taking decisions and will remain a formality except where this actually takes place. The only substantial ways in which people can be said to decide are when they participate in deciding the agendas and influence the choices that are made. Choosing between two parties who appear as if out of nowhere, and do not even say what they really plan to do, does not count as taking a decision. People need continuous access to all those contexts, inside political parties and outside them, at national and regional and local level, where they can shape the decisions that are made. The curse of the meeting then remains. But democracy also means people being regarded as equals and not more important when they go out to more meetings. Arguing for greater decentralization of decisions, John Keane says we need a variety of spheres 'in which different groups of citizens *could* participate, if and when they so wished' (1988a:13), but that people will want to make themselves heard to different degrees and on different topics. Some, presumably, will never make themselves heard at all. If participation were painless, we might well dismiss these people as having indicated by their absence that they were happy for others to decide. Since participation is in fact notoriously costly – in energy, often dignity, and time – we cannot follow this path.

Though he does not discuss the problem in these terms, John Keane suggests one possible resolution when he lists a number of initiatives on which the central government could guarantee resources, but then leave it up to local constituencies to determine exactly how these resources should be deployed. Thus the government might decide to set aside a certain amount of money for childcare, but those who chose to get involved in the local organization would be the ones to decide what form the childcare should take. This is an immediately appealing example, but the very attraction rests on a half-submerged notion of what is a basic and what a subsidiary concern. The more decentralized a service becomes, the more it will vary from one area to another – because people differ in their preferences and ideas, but also because they differ in the degrees to which they become active and involved. In each case people would have to make choices between quality and quantity (should they improve the service, or concentrate on making more places available?), and choices over the kind and range of care (should it be nurseries or childminders? should the emphasis be on learning or playing? how structured should the environment be?). Children living in different areas would then be offered different kinds of facilities, and some of these would be better than the rest.

If we accept this divergence as part of what a democracy is about, it is partly because the weight we attach to participation and choice is enough to balance the potential inequalities. It is also, I believe, because the precise form and quality and organization of childcare are not yet considered determining influences on people's lives. We more readily accept variation and experimentation here because, rightly or wrongly, most people regard pre-school childcare as a subsidiary and not a central concern. (Parents and politicians alike have proved more reluctant to delegate full responsibility to local activists when it is the organization of schools that is at stake.) When it comes to issues on which there is a stronger commitment, then the fact that a decision is being taken at an open meeting which all could *in principle* attend is not regarded as enough of a protection. People have low expectations about the degree to which they might become involved. So while they might be prepared to support direct democracy in a range of subsidiary concerns, they will prefer the control that is exercised through the vote when the decisions are ones that are 'basic'. There are always risks associated with decentralized, meeting-based decisions, and the main risk is that the activists will be unrepresentative.

If democratic equality is to mean anything, it means that a society must submit its 'ultimate' decisions to a forum in which all can take part. Realistically this means the vote, through national and local elections and, on some issues, national referendums. There may be a future scenario, when the pressures of time have been equalized between women and men and societies can afford to move up the scale and set their standards of participation a bit higher. But since gender is not the only determinant of levels of participation, this would require a great many more changes as well. For the foreseeable future, democracy has to rely on liberal minimalism for those decisions that are regarded as the more fundamental, and can only be extended by meeting-based participation for those issues thought more intermediate. That we should press for this extension in as many contexts as possible should, I hope, be clear from the arguments developed in this book. Much less clear is what principle could settle which decisions are basic and which are not, but this is because it is a question that only politics can decide.

Women's voices: women's issues The final point I want to return to hinges on the tension between feminist and republican concerns. Women have frequently commented on the spectacle of a predominantly male legislature deciding whether abortion should be decriminalized, and have noted with some bitterness that it is women who get pregnant and a woman who has to care for the child. Of all the political issues to which gender is pertinent, this is the most striking – and the relative exclusion of women from the arenas within which such decisions are made is an outrageous example of how undemocratic our democracies remain. The point is not that men oppose and women favour abortion: much of the evidence in Britain, for example, indicates that women are if anything more troubled than men by the question of late abortions, more concerned to weigh up protection of the mother against protection of the foetus, less happy-go-lucky about what abortion entails. The experiences of pregnancy and motherhood generate a complex and nuanced set of attitudes, confirmation, if any was needed, that this experience should be given more weight.

The corollary, however, is not that men should have no opinion on the issue. One of the more ambivalent side-effects of the last twenty-five years of feminist activity is the self-abasement often practised by 'sympathetic' men. Just as white liberals sometimes choose to silence themselves on issues of race and ethnicity, so progressive men sometimes abdicate their responsibilities in what they now conceive as a 'women's' concern. Accepting the incongruity in male legislation on such matters as abortion, childcare or affirmative action, they may apologize for their previous presumption, and ask women what they ought to do. One problem with this, as already argued, is that it too readily accepts that there is *a* women's position; another more pressing deficiency is that the stage may then be abandoned to those less reticent about their right to decide.

The further difficulty is the implication that only those with the experience have anything legitimate to say. Let me give one recent example from US politics. When challenged to justify his political support for abortion despite his personal moral objections, Governor Mario Cuomo has noted that 'there is an element of the absurd or incongruous in men making laws about something they can never experience – pregnancy' (cited in Wills 1990). As Garry Wills argues, this conflicts with

> the citizen values of republicanism, where everyone in the community is invited to ponder together all moral issues. We do not say, in a republic, that only the military can decide on the role of the military in public life – that only the academy can frame educational issues, that only believers can frame religious issues, and so forth. Cuomo seems to be taking an enlightened stand when he apologizes, as a man, for speaking on abortion; but it is a nonrepublican position.

Given the criticisms feminists have levelled at 'citizen values', this observation may not carry much weight, but I have argued throughout this book that it should certainly make us pause for thought. All members of a political community are formed and limited by their experiences, which is part of the argument that all these experiences should gain their voice. But any politics that looks towards change and transformation cannot leave things at that.

The classical liberal deals with such problems by establishing a region of private existence in which each of us makes her own moral or religious choices, and no one else is entitled to complain. The twentieth-century pluralist tackles it by the (usually dishonest) argument that all groups are free to contest with each other, and thereby contribute to the final result. From a perspective that seeks to reform or revolutionize the conditions of our existence, neither of these options is adequate, for each accepts the limits of experience as something we cannot overcome.

The most extreme alternative to liberal democracy is that associated with the Marxist tradition, some versions of which have anticipated a future beyond all significant conflict, where people act homogeneously as one. The arguments against this are too overwhelming to require further rehearsal, but it is one thing to deny conflict a voice and another to accept all conflicts as final. The recent feminist emphasis on difference and heterogeneity should be taken as a necessary corrective to those political theories and practices that have excluded sex (among other things) from the political stage. This should be viewed, however, as a starting point from which inequalities can be tackled and reduced. The crucial requirement is for women's political presence: which is not to say that only women can speak on 'women's' issues, that women must speak only as a sex.

As we approach the end of the twentieth century, two major developments set the scene. The first, and most dramatic, is the extension of liberal democratic practices of universal suffrage and free elections and multi-party competition – not only through the Soviet Union and Eastern Europe, but through the beleaguered countries of the once colonized world. One person one vote now looks imminent even in the most anti-democratic South Africa, while the heavy hand of military regimes and one-party states in other parts of Africa is being challenged again. Among those who have found liberal democracy weak and inadequate, there is considerable anxiety that these gains will sweep criticisms away and that, rejoicing in freedoms previously denied them, people

will forget for another generation the substance of earlier apprai-
sal. The problems feminists have raised, which build on and
significantly extend the critical analysis of liberalism, should help
to counter this risk.

The other major development is that the myths of homogeneity
are being shattered, most positively through the increased aware-
ness of gender and ethnic differentiation, more ambivalently
through the rise of religious fundamentalism and the 'new' nation-
alisms of the Soviet Union and Eastern Europe. The preoccupations of contemporary feminism are very much to the point in this
development, and they put before us some of the key questions
with which future democrats will have to grapple. Feminist political theorists have raised powerful criticisms of the abstract individual, and of the false universalities of much Enlightenment
thought, and feminists are now leading the way towards a new
politics based around diversity and difference. Some of the routes
opening up are ones I would prefer not to follow, but all of the
debate is crucial to the future of democratic thought. We have to
find a political language that can recognize heterogeneity and
difference, but does not thereby capitulate to an essentialism that
defines each of us by one aspect alone. The arguments now raging
inside feminist circles provide an exhilarating guide through this
terrain.

REFERENCES

Almond, Gabriel and Verba, Sidney 1963: *The Civic Culture: Political Attitudes and Democracy in Five Nations*. Princeton University Press.
Arblaster, Anthony 1987: *Democracy*. Open University Press.
Arendt, Hannah 1958: *The Human Condition*. University of Chicago Press.
    1963: *On Revolution*. Faber and Faber.
Banks, Olive 1981: *Faces of Feminism*. Martin Robertson.
Barber, Benjamin 1975: *Liberating Feminism*. Seabury Press.
    1984: *Strong Democracy: Participatory Politics for a New Age*. University of California Press.
Bashevkin, Sylvia (ed.) 1985: *Women and Politics in Western Europe*. Frank Cass.
Benhabib, Seyla 1987: The generalized and concrete other. In Benhabib and Cornell 1987.
Benhabib, Seyla and Cornell, Drucilla (eds) 1987: *Feminism as Critique*. Polity.
Bernstein, Richard J. 1987: One step forwards, two steps backward: Richard Rorty on liberal democracy and philosophy. *Political Theory*, 15(4).
Birke, Lynda, Himmelweit, Susan and Vines, Gail 1990: *Tommorrow's Child: Reproductive Technologies in the 90s*. Virago.
Bobbio, Norberto 1984: *The Future of Democracy: A Defence of the Rules of the Game*. Polity.
    1986: *Which Socialism?* Polity.
Bouchier, David 1983: *The Feminist Challenge: The Movement for Women's Liberation in Britain and the United States*. Macmillan.
Bowles, Samuel and Gintis, Herbert 1986: *Democracy and Capitalism: Property, Community and the Contradictions of Modern Social Thought*. Routledge and Kegan Paul.

Carby, Hazel 1982: White women listen! Black feminism and the boundaries of sisterhood. In Centre for Contemporary Cultural Studies, *The Empire Strikes Back: Race and Racism in 70s Britain*. Hutchinson.

Comay, Rebecca 1986: Interrupting the conversation: notes on Rorty. *Telos*, 69.

Coole, Diana H. 1988: *Women in Political Theory: From Ancient Misogyny to Contemporary Feminism*. Wheatsheaf.

Corea, Gena 1985: *The Mother Machine*. Harper and Row.

Dahl, Robert A. 1985: *A Preface to Economic Democracy*. Polity.

Dahlerup, Drude (ed.) 1986: *The New Women's Movement*. Sage.

Daniels, Norman (ed.) 1975: *Reading Rawls: Critical Studies on Rawls' A Theory of Justice*. Basil Blackwell.

Diamond, Irene and Hartsock, Nancy 1981: Beyond interests in politics: a comment on Virginia Sapiro's 'When are interests interesting?'. *American Political Science Review*, 75(3).

Dominelli, Lena and Jonsdottir, Gudrun 1988: Feminist political organization in Iceland: some reflections on the experience of Kwenna Frambothid. *Feminist Review*, 36.

Duncan, Graeme (ed.) 1983: *Democratic Theory and Practice*. Cambridge University Press.

Dunn, John 1979: *Western Political Theory in the Face of the Future*. Cambridge University Press.

Dworkin, Ronald 1989: The great abortion case. *New York Review of Books*, 29 June.

Eduards, Maud, Halsaa, Beatrice and Skjeie, Hege 1985: Equality: how equal? In Haavio-Mannila et al. 1985.

Ehrenreich, Barbara 1983: On feminism, family, and community. *Dissent*, Winter.

Eisenstein, Zillah 1989: *The Female Body and the Law*. University of California Press.

Elshtain, Jean Bethke 1981: *Public Man, Private Woman: Women in Social and Political Thought*. Princeton University Press.

Equal Status Council 1988: Milestones in 150 years' history of Norwegian women. Norway.

Evans, Judith 1986: An overview of the problems for feminist political theorists. In Judith Evans, Jill Hills, Karen Hunt et al., *Feminism and Political Theory*. Sage.

Freeman, Jo 1975: *The Politics of Women's Liberation*. Longman.

— 1984: *The Tyranny of Structurelessness*. Dark Star/Rebel Press, London. First published 1970.

Friedan, Betty 1963: *The Feminine Mystique*. Norton.

— 1981: *The Second Stage*. Summit.

Fukuyama, Francis 1989: The end of history? *The National Interest*, Summer.

Gatens, Moira 1986: Feminism, philosophy and riddles without answers. In Pateman and Gross 1986.

Gilligan, Carol 1982: *In a Different Voice: Psychological Theory and Women's Development*. Harvard University Press.

Gould, Carol C. 1988: *Rethinking Democracy: Freedom and Social Co-operation in Politics, Economy and Society*. Cambridge University Press.

Gould, Carol C. (ed.) 1983: *Beyond Domination: New Perspectives on Women and Philosophy*. Rowman and Allanheld.

Graubard, Stephen R. (ed.) 1986: *Norden: The Passion For Equality*. Norwegian University Press.

Green, Philip 1985a: *Retrieving Democracy: In Search of Civic Equality*. Methuen.

1985b: Equality since Rawls: objective philosophers, subjective citizens, and rational choice. *Journal of Politics*, August.

Greer, Germaine 1971: *The Female Eunuch*. Paladin.

Grimshaw, Jean 1986: *Feminist Philosophers: Women's Perspectives on Philosophical Tradition*. Wheatsheaf.

Gutmann, Amy 1985: Communitarian critics of liberalism. *Philosophy and Public Affairs*, Summer.

Haavio-Mannila, Elina, Dahlerup, Drude, Eduards, Maud et al. 1985: *Unfinished Democracy: Women in Nordic Politics*. Pergamon.

Habermas, Jürgen 1971: *Towards a Rational Society*. Heinemann.

1974: The public sphere: an encyclopedia article. *New German Critique*, 1(3). First published 1964.

Hartsock, Nancy C. M. 1983: *Money, Sex and Power: Toward a Feminist Historical Materialism*. Northeastern University Press.

Hedlund, Gim 1988: Women's interests in local politics. In Jones and Jonasdottir 1988.

Held, David 1986: *Models of Democracy*. Polity.

Held, D. and Pollitt, C. (eds) 1986: *New Forms of Democracy*. Open University and Sage.

Hernes, Helga Maria 1987: *Welfare State and Woman Power: Essays in State Feminism*. Norwegian University Press.

1988: The welfare state citizenship of Scandinavian women. In Jones and Jonasdottir 1988.

Himmelweit, Susan 1980: Abortion: individual choice and social control. *Feminist Review*, 5.

Holter, Harriet 1984: *Patriarchy in a Welfare Society*. Norwegian University press.

Jonasdottir, Anna G. 1988: On the concept of interests, women's interests, and the limitations of interest theory. In Jones and Jonasdottir 1988.

Jones, K. B. and Jonasdottir, A. G. (eds) 1988: *The Political Interests of Gender*. Sage.

Keane, John 1988a: *Democracy and Civil Society*, Verso.

Keane, John (ed.) 1988b: *Civil Society and the State: New European Perspectives*. Verso.

Lafferty, William M. 1980: Sex and political participation: an exploratory analysis of the 'female culture'. *European Journal of Political Research*, 8.

1981: *Participation and Democracy in Norway: the 'Distant Democracy' Revisited*. Norwegian University Press.

Lassmann, Peter (ed.) 1989: *Politics and Social Theory*. Routledge.

Lloyd, Genevieve 1984: *The Man of Reason: 'Male' and 'Female' in Western Philosophy*. Methuen.

Lovenduski, Joni 1986: *Women and European Politics: Contemporary Feminism and Public Policy*. Wheatsheaf.

Lovenduski, Joni and Hills, Jill (eds) 1981: *The Politics of the Second Electorate: Women and Public Participation*. Routledge and Kegan Paul.

Lukes, Steven 1985: *Marxism And Morality*. Oxford University Press.

McLeay, Elizabeth 1980: Political argument about representation: the case of the Maori seats. *Political Studies* 28(1).

1987: Towards a better democracy? Review Essay of the 'Report of the Commission on the Electoral System'. *Political Science*, 39(1).

Macpherson, C. B. 1962: *The Political Theory of Possessive Individualism: Hobbes To Locke*. Oxford University Press.

1966: *The Real World of Democracy*. Clarendon.

Mansbridge, Jane J. 1973: Time, emotion and inequality: three problems of participatory groups. *Journal of Applied Behavioral Science*, 9.

1976: The limits of friendship. In J. R. Pennock and J. W. Chapman (eds), *Participation in Politics: NOMOS XVI*, Lieber-Atherton.

1980: *Beyond Adversary Democracy*: Basic Books.

1981: Living with conflict: representation in the theory of adversary democracy. *Ethics*, 91(3).

Martinussen, Willy 1977: *The Distant Democracy: Social Inequality, Political Resources and Political Influence in Norway*. John Wiley. First published 1973.

Marx, Karl and Engels, Friedrich 1975: *Collected Works*, Vol. 3. Lawrence and Wishart.

Michels, Robert 1962: *Political Parties: A Sociological Study of the Oligarchical Tendencies of Modern Democracy*. Free Press.

Millett, Kate 1970: *Sexual Politics*. Jonathan Cape.

Mohanty, Chandra Talpade 1987: Feminist encounters: locating the politics of experience. *Copyright*, 1.

Morgan, Robin (ed.) 1970: *Sisterhood Is Powerful: An Anthology of Writing from the Women's Liberation Movement*. Random House.

1984: *Sisterhood is Global: The International Women's Movement Anthology*. Doubleday.

Moyser, George and Parry, Geraint 1987: Class, sector and political participation in Britain. *Manchester Papers in Politics*, September.

Mueller, Carol M. 1988: *The Politics of the Gender Gap: The Social Construction of Political Influence*. Sage.

Myrdal, Alva and Klein, Viola 1956: *Women's Two Roles*. Routledge and Kegan Paul.

Norderval, Ingunn 1985: Party and legislative participation among Scandinavian women. In Bashevkin 1985.
Norris, Pippa 1985: Women's legislative participation in Western Europe. In Bashevkin 1985.
Nozick, Robert 1974: *Anarchy, State and Utopia*. Basic Books.
O'Brien, Mary 1981: *The Politics of Reproduction*. Routledge and Kegan Paul.
Okin, Susan Moller 1979: *Women in Western Political Thought*. Virago.
O'Neil, Onora 1989: Friends of difference. *London Review of Books*, 11(17).
Parmar, Pratibha 1989: Other kinds of dreams. *Feminist Review*, 31.
Pateman, Carole 1970: *Participation and Democratic Theory*. Cambridge University Press.
    1975: Sublimation and reification: Locke, Wolin and the liberal democratic conception of the political. *Politics and Society*, 6. Reprinted in Pateman 1989.
    1979: *The Problem of Political Obligation: A Critique of Liberal Theory*. John Wiley.
    1980: Women and consent. *Political Theory*, 8(2). Reprinted in Pateman 1989.
    1983: Feminism and democracy. In Duncan 1983; reprinted in Pateman 1989.
    1988: *The Sexual Contract*. Polity.
    1989: *The Disorder of Women*. Polity.
Pateman, Carole and Gross, Elizabeth (eds) 1986: *Feminist Challenges: Social and Political Theory*. Allen and Unwin.
Paul, Jeffrey (ed.) 1982: *Reading Nozick: Essays on Anarchy, State and Utopia*. Basil Blackwell.
Perrigo, Sarah 1988: Women, the state and democracy. Unpublished paper presented to the Socialist Society, London.
Petchesky, Rosalind 1986: *Abortion and Woman's Choice: The State, Sexuality and Reproductive Freedom*. Verso.
Phillips, Anne 1984: Fraternity. In Ben Pimlott, (ed.), *Fabian Essays in Socialist Thought*. Heinemann.
    1987a: *Divided Loyalties: Dilemmas of Sex and Class*. Virago.
Phillips, Anne (ed.) 1987b: *Feminism and Equality*. Basil Blackwell.
Pierson, Christopher 1989: Marxism, democracy and the public sphere. In Lassmann 1989.
Pitkin, Hanna Fenichel 1984: *Fortune is a Woman: Gender and Politics in the Thought of Niccolo Machiavelli*. University of California Press.
Pocock, J. G. A. 1975: *The Machiavellian Moment*. Princeton University Press.
Polan, A. J. 1984: *Lenin and the End of Politics*. Methuen.
Popper, Karl 1945: *The Open Society and its Enemies*. Routledge and Kegan Paul.
Randall, Vicky 1987: *Women and Politics*, 2nd edn. Macmillan.
Rawls, John 1971: *A Theory of Justice*. Harvard University Press.

1985: Justice as fairness; political not metaphysical. *Philosophy and Public Affairs*, 14(3).

Rorty, Richard 1983: Post-modernist bourgeois liberalism. *Journal of Philosophy*, 80.

1989: *Contingency, Irony, and Solidarity*. Cambridge University Press.

Rosen, Andrew 1974: *Rise Up, Women!* Routledge and Kegan Paul.

Rousseau, Jean-Jacques 1968: *The Social Contract*. Penguin. First published 1762.

Rowbotham, Sheila 1983: *Dreams and Dilemmas*. Virago.

1986: Feminism and democracy. In Held and Pollitt 1986.

1989: *The Past is Before Us: Feminism in Action Since the 1960s*. Pandora.

Rowbotham, Sheila, Segal, Lynne and Wainwright, Hilary 1979: *Beyond the Fragments: Feminism and the Making of Socialism*. Newcastle Socialist Centre.

Royal Commission on the Electoral System 1986: *Report*. Wellington, New Zealand.

Rushdie, Salman 1988: *The Satanic Verses*. Viking Penguin.

Sandel, Michael J. 1984: The procedural republic and the unencumbered self. *Political Theory*, 12(1).

Sapiro, Virginia 1981: When are interests interesting? The problem of political representation of women. *American Political Science Review*, 75(3).

Sartori, Giovanni 1987: *The Theory of Democracy Revisited: Part One: The Contemporary Debate*. Chatham House, London.

Schumpeter, Joseph 1942. *Capitalism, Socialism and Democracy*. Allen and Unwin.

Siltanen, Janet and Stanworth, Michelle 1984: The politics of private woman and public man. In J. Siltanen and M. Stanworth (eds), *Women and the Public Sphere*, Hutchinson.

Skard, Torild and Haavio-Mannila, Elina 1985a: Mobilization of women at elections. In Haavio-Mannila et al. 1985.

1985b: Women in parliament. In Haavio-Mannila et al. 1985.

1986: Equality between the sexes: myth or reality. In Graubard 1986.

Skjeie, Hege 1988: *The Feminization of Power: Norway's Political Experiment (1986–)*. Institute for Social Research, Norway.

Smith, Barbara (ed.) 1983: *Home Girls: A Black Feminist Anthology*. Women of Color Press.

Stacey, Judith 1986: Are feminists afraid to leave home? The challenge of conservative pro-family feminism. In Juliet Mitchell and Ann Oakley (eds), *What is Feminism?*, Basil Blackwell.

Styrkarsdottir, Audur 1986: From social movement to political party: the new women's movement in Iceland. In Dahlerup 1986.

Taylor, Charles 1985: Atomism. In Charles Taylor, *Philosophy and the Human Sciences: Philosophical Papers Vol. 2*, Cambridge University press.

Thiele, Beverley 1986: Vanishing acts in social and political thought: tricks of the trade. In Pateman and Gross 1986.

Vallance, Elizabeth 1979: *Women in the House.* Athlone.

Verba, Sidney, Nie, Norman H. and Kim, Jae-on 1978: *Participation and Political Equality: A Seven-Nation Comparison.* Cambridge University Press.

Vogel, Ursula 1988: Under permanent guardianship: women's condition under modern civil law. In Jones and Jonasdottir 1988.

Walzer, Michael 1970: A day in the life of a socialist citizen. In Walzer, M., *Obligations: Essays on Disobedience, War and Citizenship.* Harvard University Press.

1983: *Spheres of Justice: A Defense of Pluralism and Equality.* Basic Books.

1984: Liberalism and the art of separation. *Political Theory,* 12.

Wandor, Michelene (ed.) 1971: *The Body Politic: Women's Liberation in Britain.* Stage 1, London.

Wills, Garry 1990: Mario Cuomo's trouble with abortion. *New York Review of Books,* 28 June.

Wolin, Sheldon, S. 1960: *Politics and Vision: Continuity and Innovation in Western Political Thought.* Little, Brown.

1982: What revolutionary actions means today. *Democracy,* 2.

Wollstonecraft, Mary 1975: *Vindication of the Rights of Woman.* Penguin. First published 1792.

Young, Iris Marion 1987: Impartiality and the civic public. In Benhabib and Cornell 1987.

1988: Five faces of oppression. *Philosophical Forum,* 19(4).

1989: Polity and group difference: a critique of the idea of universal citizenship. *Ethics,* 99.

INDEX

Index compiled by Sarah Ereira